Divine Decluttering

The Top 9 Secrets
For A Queen To Become
Ruler Over Her Stuff

Aimee Stricker

Divine Decluttering
The Top 9 Secrets For A Queen To Become Ruler Over Her Stuff

Book cover photo was provided with permission by https://www.vintagevibe.co.uk.

Author's photograph was taken by Maggie Habieda.

Important Information
Please read this

The intent of the author of this book is only to offer information of a general nature to help you clear physical clutter from your home, get organized and improve your emotional and spiritual well-being. This book was written from the author's heart and soul based on her own life experiences, and in a light-hearted way to help make your experience of decluttering an enjoyable one, just as hers was. You may find the practices and information provided in this book to be useful however, the author of this book does not dispense medical advice or prescribe the use of any technique as a form of treatment for physical, emotional, psychological, sexual or medical problems without the advice of a licensed, qualified physician or therapist. As each person has their own unique needs, this book cannot take these individual differences into account. The information provided in this book should not replace consultation with a competent healthcare professional. The author and publisher are in no way liable for any misuse of the material. Lighting candles and clearing the energy from spaces by burning sage is suggested in this book, but they should never be left unattended in a room and not used in the home if anyone who would be entering the space has an allergy to the product they are burning or sensitivity to smoke. Spraying lavender to freshen up the energy in spaces is also recommended and should not be used if anyone who would be entering the space has an allergy or sensitivity to this. All guidelines and warnings should be read carefully on labels for candles, sage and lavender. The author and publisher are in no way responsible for injuries or damage, however they may arise. If you choose to use any of the information in this book, the author and publisher assume no responsibility for your actions.

PUBLISHED IN CANADA
ISBN: 978-0-9958809-0-0

With love, I dedicate this book to you.

Contents

About The Author

Aimee Stricker loves sharing her creative gifts to inspire and help others. She is an Award Winning Author, Decluttering and Conscious Creating Consultant, Inspirational Jewellery Designer and has practiced as a Speech-Language Pathologist for over 25 years. Her degrees include a M.Sc. in Speech-Language Pathology and B.Sc. in Psychology. From Ontario, Canada, Aimee and her family enjoy the four seasons and spending time by the ocean in tropical weather.

To receive the accompanying FREE DOWNLOADABLE WORKBOOK for this book and for information on the variety of services and products Aimee offers, please visit www.divinedeclutteringbook.com and www.aimeestricker.com.

Testimonials

"Divine Decluttering is powerfully packed with gems of creative techniques to help you let go of clutter, embrace your self-love, honor your feminine, and transform your life and home."

-Dr. John Gray, PhD, *New York Times* #1 Best Selling Author of *Men Are from Mars, Women Are from Venus*

"This feminine powerful guide will not only enable you to rein free of clutter, but unleash your inner "Queen" full potential! Get ready to see the objects in your space in a different way, meet your inner "Queen" in the mirror, learn secrets for manifesting your desires, create a home that you love and become the most radiant woman from the inside out!"

-Graziella Baratta, Image & Pageant Expert, Dance, Performance & Fitness Pro, Certified Nutritionist, *Ms. United States 2008*

"This book is a must read if you want to let go of the clutter in your life once and for all! The process Aimee takes you through is so enjoyable, heart-centred and empowering; and the accompanying free workbook is very useful. Her "write a letter" and visualization exercises are unique and make it feel so real and exciting to want to become the "Queen" who rules over her stuff!"

-Charmaine Bryan, Image Consultant, Award Winning Speaker, Award Winning Author of *Stop Buying Clothes You Don't Wear*

"Experience your most divine journey! This book is full of powerful, practical, magical, and highly creative instructions on how you can gracefully and easily let go of your clutter, connect to self-love, get organized, and manifest your dreams. If you're ready to conquer your clutter, overcome negative habits and create your best life, you will benefit from this life-changing information!"
-Dr. Michael R. Smith, author of *The Complete Empath Toolkit*

"Aimee is a powerful, strong, passionate and loving woman that I have the pleasure of knowing and working with. If you want to have the qualities that Aimee has, then you need to read this book...now."
-Scott Schmaren, NeuroPerformanceologist, MAHC 2014 Hypnotist of the Year, *Oprah* **Guest, Co-Author of** *Stepping Stones To Success* **with Jack Canfield, Deepak Chopra & Dr. Dennis Waitley**

"Aimee has a powerful gift for seeing the higher purpose in everything. By helping you shift your perspective, she also helps you expand your awareness, level of peace, happiness and your vibration. This leads to a new way of being, as well as the opening of new possibilities for you. She truly embodies this *divinely feminine* way of being and living in the world. If you are drawn to her, trust it—she's a gifted teacher!"
-Lisa Berkovitz, Soul-Aligned Business Coach and author of the upcoming book *Let Soul Lead*

"I loved reading Aimee's book. It is a wonderful, inspirational book that is fun to read and easy to follow. I found Aimee's suggestions to be given in a joyful, imaginative way. Physical clutter often accumulates as a result of unresolved emotions, feelings and thoughts. As women, imagining we are the "Queen" of our own world is a wonderful way to help us get in touch with our inner, personal power to transform the things that are holding us back. Aimee is very generous in providing many tips and offering techniques that can be used to transform women's spaces and lives. It was also special and touching that she shared her own challenges and personal journey to becoming the "Queen" of her own life! Now Aimee shares her accumulated wisdom on decluttering and helps other women in a heart-centred way. Thank you Aimee!"

-Enzina DeAngelis, Energy Medicine/Reiki Master, Essential Oils Educator, Angel Guidance and Holistic Yoga Teacher

"Aimee's book is not just about decluttering in the physical sense, it is about so much more! For example, as she describes how you can get into your feminine, she explains many different ways to do this using some simple techniques like breathing in love and "dropping to the floor" to let go of inner struggle. I never would have thought that there would have been so many strategies to help let inner and outer clutter go! When I first met Aimee, I mentioned to her that she seemed very "feminine" which was something I admired, as I feel I live more in my masculine. I now realize that there are many ways for women who are living more in their masculine to get in touch with their inner feminine; and for sure I will be trying some of these strategies, and to also help

me declutter! I walk into my closet every day and am overwhelmed with the amount of clothes, but yet I tell myself I have nothing to wear! I didn't realize just how much clutter, physical and mental, that I actually have in my home and life. Thank you Aimee for opening up my eyes. I am now actually excited to start to purge and donate some of my physical clutter as I get into my inner "Queen" and stand in my feminine power!"
-Maggie Slider, Law Of Attraction Mind, Body and Soul Coach, Parenting Coach and Counselor, author of the upcoming book *Finding Yourself*, co-author of the upcoming book *The Change #11* with Jim Britt and Jim Lutes

"It was so hard to put this book down once I started reading! What Aimee expressed in her writing somehow got to my subconscious. I found that just after reading the first several pages, I chose to do something different and better for me in my day, and my son even noticed a difference in me! I could feel that this was written from the heart, which makes me feel that I am not alone in being in a rut with my clutter. I am so thankful that Aimee decided to write *Divine Decluttering*, otherwise I wouldn't have been able to start the process of letting go of the things in my life right now that are holding me back from being my best self!"
-M. Nagy, Insurance Inspector and a Mom

Praise For Aimee's *Divine Decluttering* Services

"Aimee's *Divine Decluttering* service over Skype has had a tremendous influence on my life. When I first came to Aimee, I was already into self development but I hadn't yet prepared my environment to align my inner and outer world. Aimee really helped me to connect from my heart rather than my mind. She had great suggestions to align my physical environment with what I wanted to attract into my life. She helped me to organize my space so that I really loved everything in my home and in the area of love, acting as if my soulmate was already living there with me. I got rid of a lot of old things that I didn't love and replaced them with things that felt really good. The biggest lesson that I learned and continue to apply is the power of our feelings, the power of coming from a heart connection, rather than taking a lot of action from the mind from a place of fear. Once I let go and relaxed into this inspired heart place, my confidence increased and I really could tap into my feminine much quicker and thus attracted amazing things into my life much easier and way more powerfully! By doing all the things that felt good to me, good things would just keep happening. I started the process in January, and by the end of May I attracted an unbelievable man into my life. I met him on vacation, and after speaking there a few times, we discovered we had met each other 17 years ago at a music camp when we were 16! This man remembered me so well and even had a picture of the two of us from that time. I later found a letter from him in a journal I carried that summer, which was so beautiful to read all these years later. We have an incredible soul connection and it's truly amazing what we feel for each other. True love at first sight and soulmates. I don't know what the future holds, but I know that radiating love and femininity brought us back together after so many years. I fully trust and have faith in what the Universe has in store for me from this point forward. It is a truly amazing story which I am grateful for every day. Aimee's strategies and ideas really help clarify what's important. She also teaches how to come from a place of letting go rather than control, how to stay in the present moment and to ask yourself meaningful questions to direct you through life. She really gives a lot of value for her time and I found the whole experience very unique and genuine. I am so grateful for benefiting from all her expertise and continue to apply what I learned on a daily basis. Aimee's serene and positive energy really makes you feel that she truly cares and wants to give and help as much as possible. I highly recommend Aimee's *Divine Decluttering* service for anyone that wants to attract their desires into their life while enjoying the process!"

-Female, Musician/International Performer, New Jersey

"Working with Aimee over Skype has been a delight for me because she makes decluttering fun, feminine, easy, and exciting! I call Aimee my "Decluttering Life Coach," because she not only helps me clean my space, but it translates into my everyday life. I used to feel extremely overwhelmed by my space, and it would make me feel depressed and

stuck. After working with Aimee, my space has improved immensely! It's a lot lighter, fresher, more organized, and it has my own style which really reflects who I feel I am. There were a lot of things in my life that needed improvement, such as my work, self confidence, and love life. With her loving, caring, femininely empowering and intelligent ways, Aimee has helped me not only transform my space, but my love life and work happiness too. She has provided insight to why and how my clutter affects my life, along with easy to follow, refreshing ways to tackle it and in a way that connects me to my feminine, which is very unique for a decluttering coach to do! Now I am enjoying the changes that it has brought me. I am a lot more confident, calm, relaxed, feel even more beautiful inside and organized because of her. Aimee is truly a joy to work with, and doesn't make me feel overwhelmed to handle decluttering tasks. I always feel comfortable to share and show her my "messy space," and she never makes me feel bad for it. Every Skype session with Aimee leaves me feeling inspired and armed to accomplish my goals. She also holds me to the task, making sure that I get things done. I have learned and accomplished so much through our sessions, she is such a great support! Thank you so much Aimee for providing the discipline, insight, how to, and inspiration that I need, to be my very best for myself, my man, and for everyone in my life! You're the best!"
-L.B., *Miss. New York* Beauty Pageant Queen

"I'd always known I had a lot of potential to accomplish great things. The problem was that I had always felt very cluttered mentally. That was reflected in a very disorganized house from my closets, to my drawers, kitchen, and even home office. I had made repeated attempts to clean up but just couldn't make significant changes. Contacting Aimee was a very significant event for me. She came over to my house and over the course of several days, we cleaned up and organized the entire space. She helped and coached me through the entire process. Strangely for me, cleaning up felt a bit stressful, but ultimately cathartic. Most importantly, I've been able to maintain the organization at home and also continue this pattern of behaviour into other aspects of my life. I can't stress enough how important having an organized home is to so many aspects of my life, and I feel that I'm more accomplished now than at any other point. Aimee helped me get the start that I needed. Thanks Aimee!"

-Male, Ontario

You May Find This Book Useful If You ...

- suffer from physical and/or non-physical clutter
- feel out of touch with your feminine radiance and want to release inner clutter
- are looking for ways to trust that you are supported in your life
- are looking for your life's purpose
- want fun, feminine, inspiring and simple suggestions to get your clutter out and become organized
- want to connect with your heart and inner voice
- want to connect with your authentic self
- want to remove obstacles from your life
- want to become a powerful manifestor
- are frustrated and seeking self-expression
- want to create sacred spaces in your home
- want decorating tips to honor different parts of you
- want simple solutions to get organized
- are living with lots of fears
- are out of your marriage and feeling alone
- want to connect to self-love
- want to learn to declutter in a way that honors both your inner masculine and feminine
- want to try a new way of looking at your life

- want to try new ways to clear the clutter from your life
- want to learn to trust in your inner guidance
- want a new way to look at the objects in your space
- want to learn powerful mirror work
- want to learn positive affirmations
- want to improve the relationship with yourself and others
- are looking for serenity
- are wanting more love in your life
- want to test out the power of your thoughts
- are looking for some magic to happen in your life
- are ready to surrender to your inner "Queen"
- are ready to make your dreams come true

Acknowledgements

Thank you to...

Rosa Greco for her creative suggestions, lovely spirit, ongoing encouragement and amazing help with all the details to get my book done and out into the world. You are the best!

Raymond Aaron for being a fabulous and powerful teacher, his fun, positive and heart-centred energy, guidance, providing so many wonderful opportunities for learning, and for writing a beautiful Foreword for me. Completing this book was done with ease because of what you taught me...thank you!

Dr. John Gray. The first book on relationships I ever read was *Men Are from Mars, Women Are from Venus,* and it has been on my bookshelf for over 20 years because I love it. As I was writing my manuscript, I thought of wanting to meet Dr. Gray one day, and it feels unbelievable to me how he showed up in my life to become part of my journey and my book. Thank you from the bottom of my heart for your kindness, and for your endorsement...it was so unexpected!

Lisa Browning for my first book editing experience, and all of her expertise and patience.

Sahir and Niezeka for their creative talent and professionalism in designing my book cover.

My beautiful clients for allowing me to be a part of their world, and for providing me with the opportunity to learn from them. This book would not have come to be if it wasn't for these divine souls. Thank you for your courage and willingness to try something different in your life.

Graziella Baratta for being my first "test" virtual decluttering client during her reign as *Ms. United States* Beauty Pageant Queen. It is quite amazing how she showed up in my life! I treasure our friendship and your beautiful spirit.

Scott Schmaren and Dr. Michael R. Smith for being powerful transformational teachers, for their guidance, encouraging me to continue to believe in my dreams, and for supporting me along my journey. I feel so fortunate to know you and love how you each appeared in my life at the perfect moment...thank you!

Monieca for her beautiful positive energy, our fabulous "creative play" times, and for encouraging me to stay on path with my dreams and writing.

Marny, Stacey, Terri, Penina, Judy and Joanne for years and years of wonderful friendship, support, time to grow together and tons of laughter!

Lisa Berkovitz, Charmaine Bryan, Enzina DeAngelis, Maggie Slider, Scott Schmaren, Dr. Michael R. Smith, Graziella Baratta and M. Nagy for their friendship, cheering me on, reading my chapters and their testimonials. You each mean so much to me.

My favorite authors and friends around the world who have inspired me over the years with their wisdom and stories. Thank you for sharing your unique gifts and your friendship.

Maggie Habieda for capturing my true essence through her lens; and Shirley Wu for preparing me to look and feel like my natural self in front of the lens. Thank you for creating the most magical day for me!

...and last but not least, thank you to those who mean everything to me:

My late grandparents, who are always in my heart and continue to inspire me in so many ways.

My sister, brother-in-law and family for their love and support.

Mom and Dad. You are the most loving and caring parents I could ever ask for, who support me through all.

My two precious and priceless daughters, Alexandra and Jessica. You are my pride and joy, my sunshine, and each growing up to become the most radiant woman.

The gentleman who found me. Feels like magic how you arrived, in your "Golden Chariot" and with your unconditional love. You lead me to the moment when it was time to birth this book, and there are no words good enough to express how much your loving support and encouragement mean to me.

...and of course:

My inner "Queen" and the Divine for choosing me to be the messenger for *Divine Decluttering.*

Foreword

As I read through Aimee's book, *Divine Decluttering*, I was dazzled. Aimee, being a mother raising two young daughters and doing her best to try to make ends meet, has always had the grand goal to share her life's passion in a book. *Divine Decluttering* was something in her mind to be far off in the future, and perhaps not even achievable. However, things did not happen as planned, and she did it! Not only did she complete her book in just three months times, but she nailed it! Aimee is a very creative soul who follows where her heart and spirit lead her. Her journey through the clutter in her own life began after the time she chose to leave her marriage. Her way out of her clutter will inspire you, and make you believe that you can create the life you want to, just as she has been doing for herself.

Aimee's intuitive understanding of how we create through energy, and how she incorporates this knowledge into the process of releasing physical and non-physical clutter, is impressive. What is most interesting and definitely unique to see in a book on decluttering is how Aimee honors the feminine in every woman. She explains how this Divine force can be transformed into decluttering power, in order to gracefully and easily let go of your "stuff." In addition, as a practicing speech-language pathologist for over 25 years, Aimee uses her knowledge in the area of communication and cleverly gives the best advice on how you can clear the clutter from your speech and thoughts to become a powerful communicator with the Universe.

The accompanying workbook that is available as a free download through her website is a wonderful gift for you. Although this book has been written for a "Queen," all "Kings" who are interested in conquering clutter will also benefit from many of the golden nuggets of knowledge found inside. May you enjoy your journey to a clutter-free life as you let go of what no longer serves you well, and surrender to following the words of wisdom found in every chapter of this divine book.

Raymond Aaron
New York Times Bestselling Author

CHAPTER 1
Confessions And Explanations

Dear Beautiful Soul,

Thank you for taking an interest in my book. I never thought that I would become an author as I always imagined it to be something so far out of reach, a huge endeavor that I would never have time for, and only meant to happen for those who were gifted writers with perhaps years and years of experience on the subject they were writing about. However, I see that the Universe had something else planned for me!

What you will be reading is what I wrote as I connected with my heart and spirit over a span of eleven weeks, and includes some experiences my clients have had working with me, along with some of my own as I decluttered my life. In a state of relaxation, the words just flowed out from me and onto the page. It was such a joyful experience and I felt energized after each writing session, no matter how long or short each one was. I know that my calling is to help women through my heart and creative gifts in order for them to create the life of their dreams. I realized that publishing a book is part of this calling.

If you are struggling with something in your life, whether it is with finances, a tough divorce situation, trying to raise your children on your own, health issues, abuse, your job or something else, and feel like you are being called to do something different than what you are doing, then try your best to honor what is being expressed to you. Listen to that quiet inner voice. Sometimes a calling may come in what seems to be the worst of times for you; however, there could be a very good reason for this.

All of my callings have seemed to come at times when I was very fragile and/or in a challenging or scary state of transition and by honoring them, magic started happening in my life. I want this for you too! My nature is very much more on the quiet side and private. However, I feel that it is more important to respect my calling and help others in this world than think of what is most comfortable for me. Therefore, I have moved out of my comfort zone to share some of my personal story, and have my manuscript published. I read that if something scares me, then it might be a good thing to try. Becoming an author scared me, and so I have done it!

Included with my book is a free workbook that you can download at www.divinedeclutteringbook.com. I created this workbook in order for you to have a quick reference guide to some of the content from here and for you to be able to write in as you become inspired to. I recommend that you read this entire book from start to finish first, print out the free workbook and then sign The Royal Contract. Even though I have put the contract right at the beginning of this book, I would like you to fill it in at the end, after reading the final pages.

Once you have signed the contract, I suggest you begin taking action to declutter, choosing wherever and however you would like to start! You can jump back and forth between all of the sections in this book to help guide you. There is no right or wrong way to the order of how you should get your clutter out. Just keep listening in to your inner "Queen" for guidance.

I put my heart and soul into what is here. I have written in a way to hopefully help you whether you live on your own, with a partner, with your children or others. Please take and use what you like and leave the rest. I am living my life's purpose unapologetically. I hope to inspire you through this book to find your soul's purpose and live the life of your dreams unapologetically too, as you release your clutter and fill yourself up with love!

I hope you in-joy...

The Royal Contract

With your invisible crown upon your head and your favorite pen in hand, please sign the contract below. You can also complete this in your free workbook that you can download at ...

www.divinedeclutteringbook.com.

I, _____ agree to take full responsibility for what I receive from my *Divine Decluttering* experience. I am ready to make the commitment of surrendering my clutter to the voice of my inner "Queen." I will connect with and listen to this Divine voice which is the voice of my truth living in my heart. By communicating with my inner "Queen," I will be connecting with self-love in order to help remove my inner and outer clutter as a first step to creating the life that I have always dreamed of. I am prepared to receive a clutter-less life and allow my home to give to me, from each beautiful sacred space I create. I will create these spaces one step at a time in my "Queendom" and imagine that they all join hands as each one comes to life, circling me with their unconditional love and support. I am trusting that good things will happen in my life when I decide to take responsibility for and take care of my thoughts, my feelings, words and actions, and connect to my inner "Queen" and self-love to help release my clutter.

I am decluttering my life for a purpose. The purpose for me to release my clutter is to/so that/because _____

_____. I will keep focused on my purpose as I take one step at a time along the way to a clutter-less life.

As I live my new clutter-less life, I imagine myself to feel _____. I will connect to these wonderful feelings as much as I can while I am in the process of letting go of my inner and outer "stuff."

I am ready for my *Divine Decluttering* journey.

The "Queen's" Signature _____

Date _____

As a special reminder of this significant time in your life, I strongly recommend that you photograph or video record each area that you plan to declutter and then again once each sacred space is created. Look at these photos and/or recordings often to continue to remind yourself that you are a powerful creator. I also want you to remember the following quote as you take steps to let go of what no longer serves you in your life, and especially at those times you may feel like giving up:

"A strong woman knows she has strength enough for the journey, but a woman of strength knows it is in the journey where she will become strong." –Unknown

Confessions

Christmas Day had come to a close. It was the eve of December 25, 2008. I had just put my two sweet daughters to bed in the basement apartment of my parents' home that I was renting, and then got into my own bed to finish writing the last chapter of my 250 page manuscript with the hopes and dream that one day it would become my first published book. I had never written a manuscript before. The longest documents I had ever written since graduating from Boston University in 1991 with a Master of Science Degree in Speech-Language Pathology were about five pages in length. They were detailed speech and language assessment reports. I did not enjoy writing. I even got out of completing a thesis for my degree by choosing to write a huge final exam instead. I never would have imagined that I would be writing something that I hoped would eventually become a book, and especially at that time of my life, which you will hear about a little later on.

When I completed my twelve months of writing I printed out the entire document and placed it in a large black binder. So many people encouraged me to turn what I wrote into a book; however, I felt that I was not ready to and instead started a business based on some of the content I wrote about. I trusted that my heart would know when the perfect time would be to do something with that manuscript, no matter how many months or years went by. And so I just let the binder sit on a shelf in every bedroom I've had in the three homes I've lived in since that time, and let it be.

Then one beautiful sunny and crisp, cold day in March of 2016 it happened... I decided to visit that big black heavy binder on my shelf and picked it up. This is a little about me, my story and what happened...

In The Beginning

I was a very quiet child and found it hard to express myself verbally a lot of the time however, I really enjoyed being creative and so my creative energy was expressed and in this energy I felt it much easier to speak. I loved playing piano and by age 13 I was teaching. I also loved being around pretty stones and beads and so one year later I opened the first beading store and birthday party business for children in my town that surprisingly became a huge success. In between all of that I somehow found that time was still open to enjoy jazz dance classes, help friends organize things in their homes and also act as their "coaches" when they wanted to become more fit. I loved to help make a difference in their lives.

I also was fascinated with science, the unseen world and how we create through energy. My amazing father with his science background always had some sort of fun science project for me to work on with him, and also started to run Saturday morning science classes in my public school that lead to science fairs. I am not surprised I was a bit of a science "geek," and even made it into the local newspaper a couple of times with my award winning projects.

As uncomfortable as I felt in my own skin, feeling it very hard to express myself, especially at times I wanted to the most, I was excited to enter high school as all my best friends were attending the same one as me. I received a new nickname there. I was now "the magician." My friends were surprised with how I could often powerfully manifest things that I wanted into my life; and it even made me scared when I could create what I didn't want too, just as powerfully. I really wasn't sure what I was doing to have this happen. All I know is that because I was not very expressive, I thought a lot; and I bet it was my intensive visualizing of what I wanted (that I could not express verbally) that made things happen.

Seeing how things showed up in my life how they did sometimes, did not always make me feel comfortable. I learned to accept feeling uncomfortable however, not just because of this, but because of how my home life was. Although I had a wonderful childhood, living in a quiet suburb just north of Toronto with my parents and younger sister, I felt often that some of the things that went on in my home were a bit out of the ordinary compared to the things that went on in my friends' homes. My amazing mother, who has the biggest heart and always supports me in all I do, was into eating very healthy and used to fill our lunch bags with some foods I remember feeling embarrassed to take out because they did not look like the regular "Wagon Wheel" treat or hot dog. I still remember the taste of some sort of dry carob and coconut snacks and heavy dark breads loaded with interesting seeds that I tried to swallow quickly before the outdoor lunch recess bell rang. It did not go well considering I also had braces to deal with.

My mom regularly had appointments in the city with a well-known naturopath and NY Times Best Selling Author, who also had several practices across the border. She decided to take me to see him one day because I complained of very cold hands and feet that started to hurt every time I went outside on really cold days. By looking into my eyes and knowing my blood type, this naturopath told me about all the things that were out of balance in my body. This was informative and interesting. He then concocted a terrible smelling tincture and said I must take it daily, and so I did. Whatever it was that I was taking, it made me feel so hot that I felt like I was aching to go running outside in the snow barefoot just to cool off!

Something exciting and different always seemed to be brewing in my family home. Sometimes I would walk through the front door after school to find an older Asian man walking around inside with a huge compass. My mother would be running from room to room with her hands full of silk plants and all sorts of decorative objects that she arranged and rearranged in every room, until the man would say it is just right; so I was introduced to the concept of Feng Shui (which I discovered this man was an expert in) very early on before it became more of a trendy thing where I lived.

On Fridays after dinner, instead of playing board games or watching TV with my family, my mom sometimes took me as her guest to her Chi Kong class that was held in the basement of the home of a master teacher. This class was saved for his "disciples" and my mom was one of those. Then on Sunday mornings instead of sleeping in, I joined my parents for early morning Tai Chi classes. My father became friends with the gentleman who taught the class, filled with at least 50 people every weekend. He then ended up becoming the producer and creator of a DVD on introductory Tai Chi, starring this teacher. My mother enjoyed Tai Chi and started to run classes in senior centres. I felt proud of her. With all that was going on in our home, the idea of how we can create and also heal through energy was well established in my belief system early on.

The Big Moves

As soon as I finished high school, in June of 1986, my family moved to the United States, to a very small, pretty town on the north shore of Massachusetts. After a 12 hour long drive in my parents' car to get there, I remember arriving late at night in the driveway of an 80 year old home made of wood, painted light green with a screened in porch on the side and a huge beautiful magnolia tree right in front. This home is where we would live for several months, while our new home was being built just one block from the ocean. I was used to living in newer homes and only lived in two homes all my life so this was a shock for me.

Not only did I have to deal with this huge change, I had to have it settle into me that we were sharing this home with three men who were over 60 years old and one cat. My little Lhasa Apso named Fluffy now had a friend and had to learn to stay out of the cat's food bowl, and I had to remember which shelves in the fridge I had access to and which ones were reserved for the men. I was allowed to take nothing with me into this home but my clothes and basic necessities, as everything else I owned went into storage. This move did not feel real for me as it felt so different from my life in Ontario. To make it easier, I kept remembering what my father told me before the drive... that change is a good thing and it will bring great experiences... and it did.

After that summer the other huge change I had was entering university. I graduated from high school one year earlier than my friends, having to speed through because of our move to the U.S. and so I felt that I was not emotionally prepared for this phase of my life. I was accepted to Boston University and the plan was to live in a dorm room since the school was much too far from my little town on the coast to travel into Boston every day. This meant that I had another move to do, but to my huge surprise I received a notice that there was no dorm room available for me. Instead, I was assigned a hotel room to live. Not only that, I was sharing that room with a girl who was a sophomore from upstate New York whom I had never met before. We lived together and thankfully got along very well and enjoyed having our room cleaned by the maid service every morning for a couple of months before we were assigned our individual dorm rooms.

To make a long story short, I moved to another university the following year and graduated with a Bachelor of Science degree in Psychology from the University of Western Ontario, and then two years later with a Master of Science degree in Speech-Language Pathology from Boston University. By the time I had graduated, I had lived in five different places during my studies, as well as having my family move back to Ontario into a new home after being in the U.S. for three years. By this point, I had become an expert packer and mover and tried to emotionally handle all the changes that I felt were happening quite regularly in my life. This was stressful for me.

After graduation in May of 1991, I flew home and moved in with my parents. I now had another new bedroom to get used to. My parents threw a beautiful graduation and welcome back party for me in a restaurant. Two days later, I ended up in the hospital. I had so much stress that had built up inside of me during the last months of school, from the pressures of studying for my final exams, being followed home by a stranger (which brought back memories of being stalked by a guy my freshman year), being driven into a dark alleyway near Fenway Park by a taxi driver after an evening of grocery shopping, moving, choosing to end a long term relationship with someone from my small town, thoughts of learning how to drive in the city after years of taking buses and subways during my studies, writing a resume and looking for places to work, that I found I developed little bumps under my skin on my forehead. I thought that this rash could be related to my stress. I decided to visit the doctor. He prescribed some pills that I had never taken before. I was hoping that the medication would help clear my skin before my party.

After a few doses, I unfortunately had a severe anaphylactic reaction to this drug. That is what brought me to the hospital. I ended up becoming the study project of the dermatology unit at the hospital, as they had never seen such a severe reaction to this drug before. My entire body was swollen. I was completely covered in the itchiest rash, and my legs and feet were totally numb and blue. I could not walk. The doctors filled my veins with cortisone through intravenous. I could feel that there was just enough room in my swollen larynx to be able to breathe and speak with effort. This to me was my near death experience. This to me was a message that life was supposed to be hard, because I did find it hard with all the changes I was experiencing over time, the pressures I put on myself to always do well at what I did, and the struggle inside of myself of not being able to express myself easily or when I needed to.

I am not surprised I became a speech therapist...we come here to teach what we most need to learn, don't we? I am not surprised that my airway became almost completely blocked. My pathway to communication and expression was being blocked as a sign of what I felt I was experiencing all my life as a quiet child. Once out of the hospital, it took about two months to recover fully. During that time, I interviewed for jobs still suffering from the horrible side effects of being on huge doses of cortisone, and the effects of later weaning from that.

Thankfully I received the job I wanted in a world renowned children's rehabilitation centre. I discovered a new passion of working with children with physical disabilities and syndromes, helping them communicate to the best of their ability. Although I loved what I was doing as a speech pathologist and found it extremely rewarding, at the same time I was somehow frustrated. I felt that I was neglecting some other part of me. I started to feel robotic in a way, always on a schedule and not making time for much else as I was tired after work.

I used to be very creative as a child and a dancer, and I started to miss that. I also sensed that my feminine spirit began to fade; however, I thought that maybe with being out in the working world now, this was just part of the natural change that happens. I could feel some sort of stirring inside of me to do something about my frustrations; however, I just got so wrapped up with my work that I ended up shoving all I felt down into myself, perhaps hoping the feelings would go away, and perhaps thinking that maybe I was wrong to be thinking how I was.

Later On

I soon fell in love, married and had two beautiful baby girls. Life suddenly got very busy since I was still working for the rehab centre, and also began my own private practice. I now had a home full of people I loved taking care of, had to find the time to take care of me, our home, and all of my clients in between running back and forth from daycare and preschools. There really wasn't time left for anything else, and I noticed that I was always leaving my needs to last and often didn't even get to them. I remember stripping from my clothes as soon I got home from work because I didn't like wearing conservative and health profession "business appropriate" kind of clothing that mostly felt so stiff, plain and restricting to me.

Eventually, I burnt out, exhausted myself from overworking, felt lost, had a closet full of clothes I did not like, felt so frustrated that I wasn't doing all I knew I loved to do (worried to not have a stable income if I tried something else), and was not happy in my marriage. So much stress had built up inside of me that I developed another sort of rash. This time it was even more extreme and covered my legs and face. I remember going to sleep with ice packs all the way down my legs and on my feet to help reduce the swelling and itchiness every night during the coldest winter months, when this thing developed. This triggered the memories of how much pain my feet used to be in as a child when I'd go outside on the coldest winter days.

As I'm writing this, I just remembered that at the end of grade 11 I suffered from a horrible case of shingles right down one leg. The doctors could not believe that someone so young could get this virus. They had nothing to give me to relieve the excruciating pain I was experiencing, along with irritation from the itchy rash that came with it. It was so painful to walk or touch my skin on that leg and I missed about one month of school. This was another sign of inner stress and worry as this happened around the time I found out we would be moving to the U.S., and that

I had to fast track through school (as Canada had 13 grades at the time and not 12 like in the U.S.). I know it affected my leg because I was scared to walk forward into my new life.

Getting back to the time of the latest rash, I tried all I could to make my marriage work and then made the decision to leave when I felt my inner voice expressing that it was the best thing to do, even though also the hardest and scariest thing I'd ever done. He was one of my soulmates. I am so thankful for the time we did share and for our beautiful children. I later understood that there was growth that had to happen inside of me, and this path that I chose to take was part of my growth.

New Beginning

Now on my own with my two beautiful girls, who were ages two and five at the time, I moved into the beautiful home that my ex-husband and I had purchased before I decided to leave our marriage. Nine months later I had to sell it in order to be able to pay my lawyer a horribly huge amount of money; so I packed everything up again and moved into the basement apartment of my parents' home. Although I was thankful to have this space and love my parents, at the same time it felt so depressing remembering that before marriage I was living upstairs.

My basement bedroom was now about 7' by 10' with a tiny widow close to the ceiling, having room for the single bed that was already there, and an old armoire that was purchased at a garage sale and looked like it came from a children's bedroom set. The blanket my mom chose to put on my bed when I arrived was one that was probably at least 15 years old and I did not like it because it was too "loud." It was covered in very bright colored hearts and I liked more muted tones on my bed. I couldn't even turn it over to not see them because there were even more on the other side of it.

There was one teeny tiny closet in the room so I had to quickly learn to cut down my wardrobe to about half of what it was and overall live with much less. I also had to get used to three guys in their mid 20s entering my apartment at all hours to get to their food pantry because my parents decided to rent out the bedrooms upstairs to co-op students. They shared my parents' kitchen upstairs; however, their food storage area was in my space below ground level. Those memories of the three men I had to live with in that old home in that little town in the U.S. came creeping back. I felt like a failure in a way, being back at home, yet so proud of myself in another way.

Even though I started to feel more at peace being out of the marriage, I still was so filled up with worry, confusion and fears that I was attracting situations in my life that gave me more things to worry, fear and feel confused about. It felt horrible and affected my health further. Then one day I woke up and thought to myself that if I created these circumstances in my life that didn't feel good, then perhaps I could create something that did feel good, if I chose to do something different. This is when my journey started with some sort of awakening.

For years I felt that I was avoiding the callings of my inner voice and what was in my heart, listening instead to what was in my head and often to others in my life to please them, instead of listening to me. So I decided that at this time I would start to do something different and listen, to really start to respect me more, finally! I decided to give myself more loving each and every day and it hit me at that moment that my name is French and translates to "Beloved." This was a very clear message to me that I needed to "be loved" by my own self more and "just be" more, instead of doing so much. I needed to love all of who I was unconditionally and detached from all else, listen to my inner voice and take the best care of me. I started living through the energy of love instead of through fear, trusting that life is supporting me instead of against me. I didn't want to believe anymore that I was here to suffer. I then changed my attitude about that blanket on my bed...I now loved that I was being covered in hearts that shouted out to me every night.

My Divine Journey

I had the urge one evening, as I sat down on my heart-covered bed in my tiny bedroom, to ask myself what I really wanted in the next year or two. At that moment I realized that I truly had complete freedom to do what I wanted as I was now single, could live wherever I wanted to and do what I wanted to, as long as I could keep up with my expenses (which was a real challenge at that time). I then decided to create a wish list, something I had never done before. I thought to myself that I would go "all out" and put down all I wanted to have no matter how out of reach it seemed or how extreme, because I realized that the worst thing that could happen would be that some things wouldn't come true!

I started to remember how as a child I could easily create things I wanted, including winning many raffles and contests just filling out ballots; so I decided to start believing in the magic of energy again, even though I didn't know exactly how things worked. I also have to admit that writing my wishes on paper was very hard to do, because I think some part of me didn't feel like I deserved or could have all I wanted. After giving it some thought, I sent love to that voice and went ahead with my writing. However, I did one thing before getting started with my pen; I put on my beautiful sparkling crown...my imaginary one, that is.

I decided that from that moment on, I was going to treat myself as a "Queen" and imagine living in a home that felt like my "Queendom." Even though living in a basement apartment was the furthest thing from what I'd imagine to be a palace, and I had brought with me everything from my marriage including my clothing I was so sick of wearing giving me constant reminders of my past. I decided that I was going to get the clutter out of my life with the purpose of recreating it just the way I wanted it, with a wish list in place. I was ready to start treating myself better in every way, and was hoping to receive the answers on how I could do this as I started this journey. I thought that if I imagined wearing a crown in my days, this would help me.

When I completed my list, I put it away and decided that one day everything would come true, and gave thanks for this in advance. I also decided that if something did not come true on the list, it would be because something else even better showed up for me. Remember to always ask for something that you want, or something even better! I then started listening in, connecting to my inner "Queen," the one wearing the crown, by spending more time in quiet so that I could hear what she was telling me.

I learned how to meditate which I found so difficult at first because my mind was constantly racing. When I was able to let my thoughts go, I was able to hear my "Queen" express to me. The content of this book is based on what I was told to do by this powerful yet loving voice, in order to become the best woman I could be and create the life of my dreams in the most cost effective way (because I was struggling financially), just by doing things within myself and in my home.

I know that learning from books is so helpful and I love to read now, yet I did not have energy or time to read at this point of my life so chose not to. I wanted this to be my personal "experiment," trusting that all of the answers could be found by connecting with my "Queen," asking her questions and also by listening to her instructions. I remembered how much I learned as a child about energy through the experiences I had, and decided that if I could shift the energy inside of me and inside of my home enough, removing everything that did not feel good inside and out, that something good in my life would happen. So my experiment began, and I decided to celebrate the beginning of a new journey, my "divine journey," by writing a letter to the Universe which I will share with you later on. Writing this letter seemed to give me some extra strength. When I was done, I put the letter away feeling that I was going to be fully supported. I was no longer alone.

The Queen's Secret

Every morning I placed my invisible crown upon my head to connect with my inner "Queen." I imagined feeling like the most radiant and powerful woman before heading out the door to work. This is when I started to notice some sort of contrast within myself. When I imagined what the most radiant, beautiful and powerful carefree woman would feel like, I realized that I really did not feel this way at all, and that all those years before I started my professional life and at the start of my marriage, I did feel better about myself. I did feel like I was glowing and radiating with self-love in a way, even though there still was a part of me that felt uncomfortable in my skin.

I then started to connect more with how I was feeling in my days and tried to match up words that went with the feelings I had. This is how I would sum up how I felt on a pretty regular basis: structured, rigid, feeling tight in my body, tired, trying to please everyone, always "on the go," stressed, reliable, on a schedule, predictable, worried, doing what I thought I "should" be doing instead of doing what I truly wanted to be doing, thinking too much, directive, in "survival" mode trying to make ends meet, nervous, feeling I have to keep working with little rest because I had to "produce" in order to support my children, not pretty and out of shape. To me, it felt more like a robot, or even more masculine.

I felt like I had lost touch with the best parts of myself that made me feel like I was glowing from the inside, feminine and powerful yet in a softer way that feels authentic to who I am. I felt like I lost touch with the parts of me that really enjoyed dancing and being free-flowing in my days, wearing clothing that felt silky soft on my skin instead of restricting, loved being creative, and doing things in my own time and not by the clock. My inner "Queen" told me it was time for a change. It was time to reconnect with these parts of myself that I lost. I realized that those parts of me got lost in my clutter. I was suffering from non-physical clutter. I couldn't see most of the clutter, yet I could feel it.

This awakening then triggered me to begin nurturing and honoring those parts of myself that connected me to what I felt was my feminine. Even though I felt that during the day as I worked I was still very much in my masculine kind of "take charge" energy (which is important to be in for certain things each day), I would come home and make it a point to shift into my feminine, doing some very fun things to make this happen. I started to believe that it is really important to connect with and express all of my parts in order to feel free within myself, and to love all of who I was and what I was doing both unconditionally and unapologetically. I needed to start loving myself again through my feminine.

What I found was that when I got into my feminine I felt different ... more beautiful inside (no matter what I actually looked like after my day or what shape my body was in), graceful, sensual, grounded, present, relaxed, slower paced, powerful, peaceful, connected to my creativity and to source energy. As I felt this each day, I found it easier to release the clutter that was sitting around in my space. This allowed me to begin creating a home that felt like mine, and something I loved to be in. As I did this, I started feeling even better and more excited about the items on my wish list. I even started yoga classes and writing in a journal about what I was experiencing each day as I listened in to my "Queen," and did what she told me to do. I had the urge to dance again and design jewellery just as I did years back, and so I did. The most wonderful thing was that no matter how exhausted I was at the end of the day, when I would create a piece of jewellery or get up to dance, my energy came back! That is what happens when you feed your spirit! I am looking so forward to seeing what happens when you start letting go of your clutter and allow for your soul's expression!

The Divine Wish List

After living for some time trying to take the best care of me, remembering to always wear my invisible crown, and staying in my feminine as much as I felt I wanted to each day, I found it easier and easier to get rid of things in my space that I no longer needed; things for example that came from my marriage that I really no longer had use for and stirred up emotions I really didn't want to focus on anymore. I also got better at saying "no" and stopped over committing myself so that I was not always doing things in a state of exhaustion. I also could feel that my energy shifted in divine ways that made me feel open to receiving.

Over time, I let go of a lot of clutter, and in its place surrounded myself with items that I loved, and things that reminded me of the dreams and desires on my wish list. I also started taking inventory of what I was thinking about and did an analysis of my own speech, to figure out how I could improve my utterances and the words I said, in order to feel my best. And do you know what happened within one year? Just about all of my wishes on that wish list came true! I could hardly believe it myself! It truly is amazing how my dreams became my reality so easily, while I was feeling like the "Queen" of my life, and staying present. When I realized that it truly was incredible that so many huge shifts magically happened for me in such a short amount of time, I decided that it was time to write about what I was doing. This is how my first manuscript came to be. I also decided to start a little business to help others remove the clutter from their life, and this is how my new business "Divine Decluttering" got started!

Below is a list of some of my wishes from the start of my journey. As I wrote each one I visualized and connected to how it felt having that wish come true, and I wrote down all of the details about what it was I wanted for each item and why. Here is the list:

1. To work half the time for double the pay as a speech therapist, and have less than a 15 minute commute to clients.

2. To have women who are connected to their inner radiance and who love taking care of themselves like a beauty pageant queen (that came to mind as a fun thought as I wore my crown, even though I had no connection to pageants) be interested in whatever business I create.

3. To have the perfect home show up for my daughters and me at the time I am ready to continue my journey "above ground."

4. To hire a private trainer at an affordable price, to help get me back into good physical shape.

5. To get my health back and have all body rashes, eczema and acne disappear for good.

6. To have some sort of creative business around my passions, including home organizing, helping people and jewellery making.

This is what happened for each wish, most happening within a year. Number 1 is referring to number 1 above, etc.:

1. I was interested in enquiring about becoming a speech therapy consultant for a private company I had heard about, to work in

schools in the area where I lived; however, I was too nervous to take the step to visit that office or even to write a resume to apply for work. I later attended a speech therapy conference and a woman walked up to me, asked if I was Aimee, then handed me her card and asked me to call her. I looked at her card and noticed that she was the owner of the private company I wanted to visit! She hired me, and so I left my job of 18 years. I was now working for half the hours, driving very short distances to clients and receiving double the pay.

2. The reigning *Ms. United States Beauty Pageant Queen* contacted me through a strange and unexpected series of events and asked for my help to declutter her living space over Skype (as she lived in New York). She became my first virtual decluttering client.

3. We moved into the most perfect home with all details I imagined there, on the exact street my girls and I wanted to live on. My real estate agent said that there was not a home available on that street to rent. I decided to reject what the agent told me after he showed me several others in the area. A few days later I decided to take a drive down that street I wanted to live on. I just happened to see a sign for a home to rent on that street that looked perfect. I then made the call myself to set up a visit time, and shortly after, I signed the contract to rent that place. The number of the house just happened to be the number on my oldest daughter's baseball hat she was wearing all year.

4. *Ms. United States* asked if I would be her first virtual "Bikini Boot Camp" client, so I now had a personal trainer working with me a couple days a week for some time who helped get me back in shape at no cost.

5. After a few months of taking better care of myself, I decided to stop taking all medications for the eczema, rashes and acne, and they all disappeared.

6. I created a fun jewellery business to be my hobby as I loved beading, and also a decluttering business that I started to do part-time as I still worked as a speech therapist.

My wishes had all come to be my reality!

Moving forward to the middle of 2015, I started to feel strange powerful forces inside that kept me awake at night and made me feel like I had to go through a whole new "letting go-of-stuff" experience, making sure that all the old energies from my more recent past were out of me, and making sure that even more physical clutter was released. My intuition was telling me to prepare myself as best as I could to receive something new in my life, and perhaps someone new; so I did this and when I sensed I had done enough, I just "let go." It felt really good to let go, just as it feels really good to let go of clutter. I let go of control of what I wanted in my life, chose to feel like I had everything already and allowed the Divine to step in and do the rest to take care of me and my dreams.

As I sunk into my feminine I could feel my heart open to receiving, and I felt comfortable with the uncertainty and the unknown because I had faith. This allowed me to go about my days staying present and taking the best care of myself; staying focused on me, my family and doing things that made me feel good. I just practiced the same kind of thing as I did several years back, at the start of my journey.

It then happened that just a short time later, I did receive both something and someone new! The gentleman I could feel inside of me found me. I sensed that he may be from one of the farthest places from me in North America and he is. This felt magical and the interesting similarities between us, including our histories and very unusual and highly unlikely coincidences, were fascinating to discover. What is really interesting is that he said that I showed up in his life right after the moment that he had "let go." We both had let go and because we did, we both received. It was also so beautiful to hear how strongly he energetically felt the divine feminine in me radiate out to meet the divine masculine in him.

This divine gentleman encouraged me to take my dusty manuscript that I had written so many years back off the shelf and to start writing again. I could feel something inside of me light up when he said this, and so I knew that this was the time. As I opened my large black binder and looked through the 250 pages of my manuscript, I felt that I did not want to go back and edit what I had written and create a book from that; so instead, I started from scratch. As I wrote, I felt the words appear through my heart and spirit, and the pages receiving them. I was in my zone as I wrote and it felt effortless to do. It was just surprising to me that the calling to write again happened to be at the busiest time of the year for me. My schedule was so full and I was not sure how I would fit in writing time. I did not allow that to become an excuse to move forward though. I felt that if a calling came, it was time to answer it and time would show up. I believe linear time to be an illusion and something we can expand; so I wrote and had all the time I needed for this. The words all flowed out onto the page and have now flowed into your hands.

Now it is your turn to experience your most divine journey; and you are going to begin yours the same way that I began mine...with a wish list. It is your time to dream big and prepare to make your wishes come true! When you are ready, please use my free workbook that you can download at www.divinedeclutteringbook.com to write down your greatest longings and wishes.

Connect with all of your senses for each one and visualize in as much detail as you can. As you write down each desire you have, also write down WHY you want each one. This will be a powerful exercise to help you connect on a deeper level. When you have completed that, describe what you expect to FEEL as you are living each wish as if each has already come true. Then really connect with and feel those emotions. This I believe, is the most important step to complete because we attract things to us that match how we feel. When you are done, give thanks in advance to the Universe for making your wishes come true or bringing you some things even better. Then "let go." Let this be your first experience in practicing detachment. This is a powerful exercise; just believe and trust.

Getting Clear On Clutter

Now that you have completed your wish list, do you feel that you are truly ready to receive your best life? I imagine you are, or you would not have picked up this book to help you! Now that you know a little about me and the clutter I suffered from in my life, it is time to look at your own life... Do you feel you have *received* clutter in your life, or is it that you feel that your clutter has *received* you and has now consumed you to the point that you can't breathe as easily because of the stress that has built up inside of you from all of it? Do you feel that you can't move around in your home in your most divinely free feminine spirit because the clutter is blocking the flow, as you move from space to space, and also creating blocks to your own inner flow? Or are you feeling so weighed down from your clutter that your body feels heavy and does not have the desire to move in the most beautiful elegant ways that you are gifted to move in order to feel your best? Do you feel you are able to take responsibility for the clutter you own? I suggest that you do start to take responsibility if you have not yet, because I do not see you as a victim of your life. I see you as a powerful creator able to design and create the life that you want, just like I have and am continuing to do.

I also am recommending that from this moment you begin to feel really good about the clutter you have accumulated; because if you have the power to create a clutter-full life, you also have the power to create a clutter-less one. I believe we create based on what our beliefs are and what we focus on, and now that you will be focusing on becoming more and more uncluttered using the tools I describe in this book, you will powerfully change your situation.

Let's begin with my definition of clutter. Clutter can be defined as anything that you do not use, need or want that takes up room in your personal physical spaces and inside of you. It drains your energy and affects the serenity you are meant to feel in life. Some areas in your home may look neat and organized and you may even receive complements from those who visit, that you keep a beautiful space, yet to you it feels cluttered because of how you feel when you look at what you have in your surroundings. You do not feel at peace.

I believe that an important aspect of living our best life is feeling comfortable in our homes and nurturing ourselves in one that supports us in our life's purpose, and to do this the clutter must be cleared out. It feels so good to replace useless items in a home with useful ones and replace useless nonphysical clutter with healthier choices, and I want you to experience this. Physical clutter refers to the objects you have in your physical spaces. The non-physical clutter can be found in several places including in your mind, your beliefs, your habits, schedules, the words you express and in your electronic devices. I will address all forms of clutter very simply in this book and in a way that I hope inspires you and gets you excited to take action.

My signature method that comes from what I experienced in my own life will show you how to access your beautiful "Queen" power and creative energy, to be able to gracefully and easily let go of the clutter from your inner and outer spaces, and to express all of who you are. What I found is that by giving myself permission to live more fully through my feminine, and also do things through my masculine in a way that feels good (because both are important to honor and express through, as they divinely dance together), I am able to easily let go of "stuff" whenever it happens to accumulate. It also makes me feel like I am taking care of my heart and soul as I express myself through my feminine and I wish the same for you. I want you to feel radiant, connected to all of you and filled up with love so that you have lots to share with everyone in your life. I feel that as a radiant "Queen" it is important to live your life authentically, feel and express all the parts of you, and love living and expressing through your masculine and feminine in whatever ways feel best to you. I hope that through what you learn here, you begin to enjoy decluttering in a way that honors both your divine masculine and divine feminine and makes you feel like a beautifiul "Queen" who takes the best care of herself inside and out.

As you clear what you don't need from your life and connect to your inner "Queen," I hope you also come to discover your passion, your purpose, and all you desire that may have been buried under all of your "stuff." Also, when you give your inner and outer home and those in your life the gift of unconditional love and attention from your open heart, then you open yourself up to receiving the most beautiful life.

Everything is energy, and so as you make great changes in your inner and outer home, you will experience great changes over time in your life. As women, we are very good givers and providers however we often have a hard time receiving. I can imagine that you are tired of giving and giving and receiving nothing or very little back. I want you to start to feel like your home and what you have inside of it is giving to you, and that you are open to lovingly receive what it has to offer in the creative ways you discover it can give to you, as you read through this book. Are you ready to receive a clutter-less life? Are you comfortable with receiving something better for yourself? Do you know how to open yourself up to receiving something better?

I am going to give you the tools you need so that you do stay open to receiving the gift of an uncluttered life. I also hope that from my suggestions, that you will also learn how to stay open to receiving all else you desire! You are the "Queen" of your life and every "Queen" deserves to live in the most nurturing beautiful "Queendom" and have all she wants! If you are ready to receive this, then with your gorgeous crown upon your head please continue reading and let's get started...

The Letter

Do you remember the letter to my higher power that I wrote and mentioned earlier? Following is part of that letter:

Dear God/Universe/Divine Power,

I am surrendering to the voice of my inner "Queen," which I believe is connected to you. Please protect me, the man of my dreams and my beautiful children throughout my journey. Please give me the strength and everything I need, to go through my healing to become the happiest and most clutter-free person I know I deserve to be, and want to be. Please also give me the strength to collect all that I learn along the way to be able to share, so that I can help so many other women around the world sometime in the future.

I am now going to focus on giving unconditional love to myself and take care of all my needs first, as well as those of my children of course. I am now choosing to see everything I bring into my life, that I believe I do in partnership with you, as a gift and opportunity to learn from. I am ready to receive my best life and am going to learn how to stay open to receive this. I live in appreciation and am full of thankfulness, always.

All My Love, Aimee

If this letter is something that resonates with you and you see how writing something similar may add to your journey, now may be the perfect time for you to pick up your pen. There is space to write your letter in my free workbook that you can download at www.divine declutteringbook.com.

Now that you know your purpose for decluttering your inner and outer home and are prepared with your crown upon your head to do so, you are ready to take the next step. The next step is to make several divine commitments. If you are ready to be presented with these commitments, I welcome you to take an elegant walk into the next chapter...

CHAPTER 2
You Will Make These 12 Divine Commitments

To begin, I am providing you first with twelve recommendations that I feel will help make your decluttering journey a smooth one. I suggest you review these commitments on a regular basis as you declutter, until you feel you are practicing each one of them comfortably. I want you to be feeling at your very best as you clear out everything from your life that is no longer serving you well. As you practice what is described here, I assure you that you will begin to feel better and better about yourself and as you do, you will have a much easier time letting your clutter go. Choose one commitment to practice first, and keep focused on it for an amount of time that feels good for you such as a week, or until you feel you have it mastered. Then move on to another one. These twelve are listed in my free workbook that you can download at www.divinedeclutteringbook.com in order for you to keep track of those you have started to practice, and for note-taking.

To Take Care Of Yourself First

If you could only remember one commitment, I suggest that it be this one. Doing something good for yourself first is part of what I call "healthy selfishness," and something that is necessary to live the life of a

"Queen." In order to be at your best for others, you must take care of yourself first. You cannot serve from an empty vessel. You must fill yourself up first with what you need in order to feel and be at your best. Taking care of your needs first is part of self-respect and when you do this, you will be in a much better energy to take care of others' needs.

To do something good for you first can be something as simple as resting on the couch to catch your breath for five minutes after a long day at work while you cuddle with your children, instead of running right into the kitchen to make dinner feeling totally exhausted. Remember what the procedure is in the airplane – put your oxygen mask on first before placing one on your children. Here are some other examples of how you can take good care of you first:

- making your bed as soon as you wake up
- eating a healthy meal before checking emails
- creating a relaxing morning routine for yourself before everyone else gets up, such as starting with a meditation, journaling, speaking in the mirror
- allowing voice mail pick up your calls when you are tired and need to rest
- rescheduling an appointment or time out with friends when not feeling your best, so that you can rest
- putting all dishes in the dishwasher/clearing the sink of dirty dishes before rushing out the door so that you come home to a clean kitchen

Use your workbook to write down some things that you will practice as part of "healthy selfishness."

To Obey The Rules Of The Road

I've chosen the word START for you to remember the first letter of each of six important practices to incorporate into your daily routine.

Show Up In Your Crown

If you want something to change in your life, you have to show up to make the change, so do this wearing your crown! When you show up ready, you are also telling the Universe that you are ready to receive its support. Procrastinating is not showing up. If you do procrastinate, examine the reasons why you do this. I know that for me, I delay starting tasks when I am fearful that perhaps I may not do the best job at it or if I need support, but am scared to ask for help. You have to also sometimes wonder if the reason you put off doing something good for yourself is a form of self-sabotage – not allowing yourself the pleasure to feel happy about something you know you can accomplish. Listen to how you express an utterance, because if you say something that contains the word "but" for example, after you express what it is that you want (e.g. "I want to write a book, but I have no time to."), that second part of the sentence may be your fear talking. Listen to the first part of your sentence and let the rest go. If you truly want something, you will make it happen by taking inspired action. You will then see how the Universe magically shows up for you and also does the "figuring out" part. When you choose to show up for what it is that you want, trust that you will be fully supported, and that the time you need to do what you want will show up too.

Take One Divine Action

It doesn't matter how long you spend doing it, but commit to pick ONE thing to declutter each day. It could be something as small as throwing out an old magazine or as big as a ten minute decluttering experience in a drawer. Remember that as you divinely declutter one thing each day, you are clearing the way for all that you want to come to you. You can think of your clutter as a brick wall that stands between what you want and where you are. Start removing the bricks one by one and get ready to experience the magic that happens!

Assign A Royal Place

New items that come into your home each day must be assigned a space to live in immediately (and one of these spaces may also include the trash can) including all mail, papers and anything that snuck into your pockets, wallet and purse.

Remove The Rubbish

For each new item you bring into your home, you will get rid of the same number of items and do it that day, so that the clutter does not build up further. For example, if you purchased a new blouse, go into your closet and choose one that needs to be let go of. If there isn't one, then find another piece of clothing to remove from the space. If you purchase a new kitchen utensil or tool, find one that you no longer need and get rid of it.

To Put Back What You Take Out

Whenever you take something out, be sure to put it back right when you are done using it (e.g. tools, art supplies), wearing it (i.e. clothing) or consuming it (i.e. food and drinks). Also teach this to your children and set a good example by practicing this habit yourself first.

You show yourself respect when you listen to what your body is expressing to you, and then take the action that is necessary to deal with what comes up. A long time ago I remember someone mentioning the word HALT to me as an acronym, to help me remember some important things. I have included this acronym here so that it may help you too (and just added an S to the end). You must slow down and take a break from decluttering when you feel: **H**ungry, **A**ngry, **L**onely, **T**ired, **S**ad.

Respond to what your heart and body are crying out for. When hungry, eat something nutritious; when angry or sad, connect to the emotion instead of stuffing it down, pretending the feeling will go away. Take it out, see it, hear it, feel it, express it in a healthy way and give it the acknowledgement it deserves. You are loving yourself when you do this.

If you place a positive thought or affirmation on top of your angry or sad feelings such as, "I am feeling happy and calm," then I would call this kind of positive thinking in this moment, "clutter." Just sit with "what is." Be present with yourself. When really sad, overwhelmed or confused, you may even feel that you want to drop to the floor or onto the bed. Let it all go...drop to the floor, express and surrender. You will feel yourself come into your feminine (which I will discuss in the next chapter) as you do this, which may feel beautiful for you. Be with the emotion and where you feel it in your body. Breathe in deeply and relax into that place inside of you where you feel the emotion affecting you the most. Allow for its full expression. Your body will begin to relax as you release everything from inside, and you will experience a shift in how you feel.

When lonely, reach out to a friend or family member. When tired, take a moment to close your eyes and rest. As little as ten minutes of slow deep abdominal breathing, resting on the couch with your eyes closed, feeling your body and mind letting go of all the stress, can make you feel really refreshed.

You will commit to STOP any decluttering task BEFORE you get tired. If you continue to declutter while exhausted, your mood will start to shift, making the end of your amazing session of clearing things out not feel as good as it could have felt. You may start to have fearful thoughts creep in as you get tired to make you doubt yourself and what you are doing. You want to leave each decluttering session feeling great and excited for the next time you take action, so this is a very important rule to remember.

Use your workbook to write down some new rules of the road that you will try.

To Stay Open To Receiving Support

You have chosen to undergo a significant change in your life, and it is important to be open to receive support at times of change. Growing up, even though I came from a very supportive home, my soul seemed to believe that I had to figure out things on my own and if I asked for help, it would mean that I would have failed in some way. I carried this belief into my marriage and I made my life extremely difficult because of this. When I finally prayed for help, after I decided to separate, help arrived like a miracle had just occurred in my life and in very interesting ways that made me feel like I was a character in a bizarre movie.

The problem though, was that I could not trust the help. I was not used to receiving support and was extremely skeptical to trust anyone who wanted goodness for me. I eventually learned how to trust, and it started with me learning to trust myself first, my inner voice and my choices. Over time, I began to feel that the more I trusted myself, the more I could trust others.

You may find the affirmations below helpful and comforting to have if you are not used to receiving support in your life. As you read or state each one, connect with the feelings you had from a time in your past where you felt supported in something. It does not even matter if it was when you were a child if you can't think of a time as an adult. This will help attract to you an experience that brings on similar feelings or perhaps even better ones! Remember that we attract things to us that match how we feel.

"I choose to be supported in my life."

"I am worthy of receiving support."

"I ask for help when I need it."

"As I undergo change, I surround myself with support."

"I appreciate and am open to receiving support in my life."

"When I choose to help myself, I attract supportive people and experiences into my life."

"People want to help me."

Use your workbook to write your own statements and/or the ones you like from here.

I hope that you find me as your really strong support person as you continue to read through these pages and take action, because I really want to be! Carry this book throughout your days if you need to...in your car, your purse, your briefcase. Keeping a favorite self-help book with you as you go about your day may feel comforting to you and something nice to refer to at times when you feel lonely, or need some reassurance that everything is going to be ok.

To Stay Perfectly Present

If you want to become the most sensual feminine woman then I suggest that you stay present as much as possible with yourself and with others. Be present with your emotions instead of shoving them down or hiding them as you put on an act of feeling better than you truly do. Acknowledge your thoughts, be aware of what is in your surroundings, and connect to those you speak with right where they are at. When you connect, do it with warm eye contact and energy that comes from your heart. When you declutter, I want you present with the objects in your hands. You will give them the respect they deserve and take care of them in the best way you see fit.

Use your workbook to describe some moments you plan to be more present in.

To Know What You Can Change

So often we get angry, frustrated and sad over things that we have no control over and cannot change. Think of how much of your time is spent dwelling on someone else's poor behavior that makes you upset, the weather, the job market. Think about how much time you spend thinking of ways to try and fix your partner. I want you to think of your mind as your home with lots of small rooms. How many of your rooms are filled with thoughts that connect to what you have no control over and cannot change?

When I started clearing out my rooms, I thought that it would be easier for me to clear things out by listing on paper what I wanted changed. I then came up with the lists you will see below. I was so relieved when I could clearly separate what I had control over and what I could not control. Knowing what I could not change in my life allowed me to free up lots of rooms, as I let go of thoughts connected to those things. Having more free space in my mind, I received more peace; and time in my days all of a sudden opened up as I had fewer things to obsessively dwell over and try to fix.

These Are Some Things That You Can Change

What the rooms in your home look like

Your personal possessions

How you see yourself

How you take care of your home

How you take care of your body

Every choice you make

How you manage your energy and your emotions

Your thoughts

Who you bring into your life

Things you bring into your home

Connection to the power greater than yourself

Your intentions

Your actions

Your words

Your beliefs

What you choose to spend your money on

Your food choices

Your sleeping habits

These Are Some Things That You Cannot Change

Nature and the weather

How others see you

The final result of your body

Someone else's choices

The feeling and mood you just experienced

Who the population is made of

What is in the news

God/Your Higher Power

The time on the clock

What happens as a result of your intentions and thoughts

What happens as a result of your actions

What happens as a result of the words you express

What happens as a result of your beliefs

Use your workbook to write your lists and what you will do to take action.

To Take Responsibility

From this moment on, you have the choice to not see yourself as the victim of your life. What you focus your energy on expands. Everything is energy. You attract things into your life based on your unconscious beliefs and how you are feeling. Your feelings come from your thoughts, so it is important to be aware of the thoughts you are thinking. Also, if you are able to take time to look at your unconscious beliefs, identify which ones are not serving you well and then change those beliefs, you will see shifts happen in your life. It is important you start to recognize the beliefs that may be holding you back from having your best life, let them go and put healthy supportive beliefs in their place. You may need to seek professional support to help you with this.

Use your notebook to write down the beliefs you feel you have that may be holding you back from clearing out your clutter. Under each belief, write down a new one that you feel will help and support you to create the living space and life you want.

To Love All Of Who You Are

You are a beautiful woman from the inside out. I want you to feel like you are sparkling and radiating with love that begins inside of you as you take action to clear your clutter out. Part of self-respect is loving who you are. Be gentle on yourself, and remember to unconditionally love every part of you. Not only do I hope you begin to love all of who you are as you practice all I suggest in this book, I want you to love everything that you have in your personal space. You are going to love all items you keep in your home and everything that you have inside of you...meaning your thoughts, beliefs, feelings and habits. I bet that you will even start to make smarter choices around what you eat and drink as you learn to love and take better care of you in every way.

Use your notebook to write down a part of you that you feel you can love more.

To Always Tell The Truth

To live as a divine being you must tell the truth. To be true to yourself and to attract honest people, you must speak the truth yourself. Think of a mirror. What you radiate out is what you receive in return. Think of how the Universe responds to your expression. As your subconscious mind takes everything to be true, and does everything in its power to make you a truthful and honest person, you must be careful with your thoughts and words. So, for example, if you call in sick to work but truthfully, you are just not in the mood to go in, your subconscious mind may start to work with the energy of the Universe to attract to you an illness because it takes everything as true and wants you to be innocent. During this journey, please be truthful to yourself and speak the truth. The only one you will be cheating is yourself, if you are not honest or expressing/thinking of things that do not feel good to you. Work through this book in an honest way.

To live a fulfilling life, it is also very important to listen to that quiet voice within, as this voice is your truth. This is the voice of your "Queen" self, and the one that is connected to your Creator and it will be up to you to listen to it, trust and believe in it, and follow it.

Use your notebook to describe what you will change, so that you feel to be your best honest self.

To Be Flexible

You have chosen to consider trying a new way to manage the clutter in your life, because you are reading this. That is a great first step! See yourself as flexible and wanting to change some of your ways. As you read, pay close attention to what makes you feel uneasy. Notice which suggestions in this book, you feel that you do not want to try. Think of why this may be. Connect with how your body feels, if you sense some sort of resistance as you read. Practice letting go of this resistance. There is beauty in doing this. Feel how your body relaxes when you choose to say "yes" to being flexible, and as you open yourself up to trying something new.

"I stay open to trying new ways to remove the clutter from inside of me, and inside my home."

Use your notebook to write statements you feel will help you to stay flexible.

To Be Patient

The world was not created in one day. Your clutter-less world and all you desire on your wish list, may not be created in one day either. You are creating in partnership with the Universe, everything that comes into your life. Practice patience as you declutter. I get the feeling that there is always some sort of catch up time. You may do a lot of work clearing clutter from an area in your home, your schedule, and in your mind for example, and be waiting for something to shift for the better in your life. Let go of expecting anything.

Instead, choose to stay present. Know that something that feels good to you will happen at some time, from the decluttering that you did, because everything is energy. This means that even a small amount of sorting and releasing that made you feel better than you felt before you took action, will bring some sort of change to your life because you shifted your energy.

If you notice that nothing has changed in your life since you decluttered in quite a large way, allow for this lull and know that when nothing is going on, when you feel some sort of flatness inside, that your partner is at work for you. Breathe in love. Let go of worry. Feel yourself being accepting of the uncertainty and the unknown. Stay present and thankful for what you have in your life right now. See this time as the "cooking" time. Remember to stay away from the stove and do something else, while your creation is being prepared. Don't interfere in the process.

Don't sabotage yourself. Don't go back to your old ways and habits. Relax and stay present in your day. When you have the biggest flat period, imagine and trust that the biggest gift will be coming to you. The Universe will bring to you what you need at just the right moment; so please be patient.

Use your workbook to write down some things you enjoy and will do instead of worry.

To Love The Light

Start each day by opening your curtains and some windows to allow the light and fresh air in. Do this in all of your rooms. Allow the energy of the Universe and the sun to shine on you and your space. You are growing a beautiful space inside now like a garden. Make sure that you give your garden the light it needs, in order to feel nourished. The other important element you need in order to grow a beautiful garden is water. Make sure you drink water throughout your day. You may find that when you are fearful and worried, that your mouth gets dry, and you are more thirsty than usual. Make sure you stay hydrated.

It is also critical to turn the soil in your garden in order to grow a healthy one. Like the soil, you should keep moving too. When you move, you change your energy; when your energy changes, your thoughts and feelings change too. Get up, go out, stretch, walk, dance, do anything to get yourself moving and active during a part of each day.

Use your workbook to write down what you will do to honor the light in your home and the physical activities you will try, in order to change your energy.

To Always Be Grateful

The idea of being grateful or thankful is so important. I feel it is important to thank our Creator for what we receive, as if everything is a gift; even if we are not so pleased with what it may be. Perhaps there is something that we are to learn from those times we are not pleased with what comes into our life. You may choose to believe that nothing comes to us by coincidence, and that we create every experience we have. This may help you believe that you are a powerful creator of your life experience.

I believe that we attract things to us based on our thoughts, beliefs and feelings; and it happens in such amazingly accurate ways sometimes, and need to be thankful for this. Ok, so you have a huge mess in your life right now and you cannot accept the fact that everything you have is a gift, but I believe that it is. You have it all for a reason. In fact, the more clutter you have, the more thankful you may want to be, because it is just more proof that you are powerful and have been able to bring in to your life what you thought about. Perhaps you have been thinking a lot about how much "stuff" you have to remove from your surfaces, and as a result you received more of it. Maybe you have been thinking about all of the single socks and unworn pairs in your drawers, and you received even more. Or, perhaps you have been thinking about how critical your boss has been lately with you, and you then received more criticism.

I know that you have also created some wonderful experiences in your life, and you will have more as you start to take action with what is suggested in this book. Many wonderful experiences are coming your way along with a wonderful clutter-less home!

Use your workbook to write down at least seven things that you feel thankful for, that are related to the clutter you have. Then make the commitment to write a list each day, of several things you are thankful for in your life and why you are thankful for each. This exercise can help to create miracles in your life. It is one of my most favorite things to do each day!

Here is something else fun to visualize in order to get you motivated and excited. Imagine that you have a very handsome butler (you are a "Queen," remember!), and he has entered your home wearing his white gloves. See him placing all of your clutter on a beautiful silver platter. How large of a platter would you need to fit everything? Imagine your butler now holding the filled platter (no matter how large it may have to be), and lifting it up so that it magically comes in contact with the stars. Next, see him tipping the platter over slowly, and everything on it floating away into space. Imagine your things now on a journey to their new owners or spaces to live in. There are people and places waiting to receive what you released. How does this make you feel? Do you feel as if you'd want everything back? What else do you see? Do you see a beautiful shining silver platter right in front of you? Think about this platter and what it could represent to you. This is your gift—the silver platter, ready to be seen, enjoyed and used. Look into the shining platter. Can you see yourself, now that your clutter has been removed? Be thankful for who you are and what you have in your life at this moment. Accept all of who you are and "what is," through your loving compassionate eyes.

Now that you have visualized seeing yourself in the reflection of your shiny silver platter, you are ready to meet your most radiant feminine self! You will find her in the next chapter...

CHAPTER 3
You Will Understand The Royal Essentials

Your Essential Feminine Flow

During your decluttering journey, you will only choose to keep those items in your personal space that your inner "Queen" agrees for you to keep, those items that make you feel like a "Queen" and those that align with all you want in your life. Before you get started though, I am going to help you get to the place of feeling like the most divinely radiant "Queen" from the inside out so that you are prepared to take action.

Every woman holds many different personalities and energies within her. We each are made up of feminine and masculine energies. These two energy types are two halves of the same whole in a constant dance. It is beautiful that we are each unique and express both kinds of energies in different ways and amounts. Knowing when to be in and knowing when to take action from either your masculine or feminine energy I feel, is a way to make decluttering easier, find success in life and also in love. I am sensing that you are the kind of woman that enjoys being in your feminine or are one that is aching to experience what this feels like, if you have not spent very much time in this energy. I sense that for quite some time you have lost your deep connection to your feminine which has left you feeling drained, washed out, too structured, bossy, disconnected to your authentic feelings, out of touch with your body, frustrated and perhaps also achy, desperately needing a massage. In this state I imagine you have tried to get rid of your clutter or maintain clutter-free spaces; however, have not had very much success.

It is so common for women these days to have lost touch with their feminine being "out there" in the working world, trying to pursue what they love and in the role of taking care of those they love, their partner, home, and raising children either in a relationship or as a single mom. If this has happened to you, or if you sense a block come up as you think of your feminine due to a childhood experience or something else, then you may be feeling off balance or out of touch with a very important part of who you are. You may want to seek professional support if you feel you need help moving through a block. Also, if you are not doing what you love, or do not even know what that may be or what your purpose in this lifetime is, then connecting to your feminine may be the magic that you need in order for you to awaken to this.

When you are living more in your masculine energy then you will find yourself to be task oriented, ready with your "to-do" lists, more aggressive, in your mind thinking a lot, directive, logical, living to survive and provide, rigid, directive, realistic, logical, structured and in "take action" mode. It is important to be in this energy for some things (e.g. when you know what you want and know that there is a logical sequence of steps to take to achieve what you want so you take them).

When connected to your feminine energy you will find yourself to be radiant, soft, nurturing, creative, intuitive, flexible, flowing, surrendered, living for joy, receptive, feeling more than thinking, in your heart and body rather than in your mind, doing what you truly love rather than what you think you need to do, resting and being still more, experiencing synchronicities, feeling magnetic and powerful in a different kind of way than what you would experience when in your masculine, and feeling like you will always be accepted as you decide to just "be," rather than feeling like you must achieve something for acceptance.

In your feminine, you will feel the desire to act based on an inner knowing; and you may receive ideas in a way that you could not when in your masculine, as you open yourself up to connecting with your creative spirit, intuitive guidance and source energy. You will also feel ok with not knowing everything upfront; which means being accepting of the unknown and uncertainty in your life, as you continue to trust your inner knowing. I want you to feel that you can sink into your feminine at any time, and find the best balance of your energies to make you feel connected to all of who you are and free.

This book is for those women who feel they want to reconnect to and honor their feminine and so the suggestions I give here may not be suitable for all women. I am sharing my unique experience on how I was able to clear the clutter from my life, feel better, find my purpose and make my dreams come true with the hope that I can inspire you to do the same! I naturally feel at my best being in my feminine for much of the time (and that is just me) and I feel it is part of my calling to help others who want to reconnect to theirs.

Several years ago, I received comments from a few women and a couple of men that made me feel bad about my femininity. I then started to connect being in my feminine as weak, and that I could not succeed in life the way that I was. I am thankful that after some time I chose to let go of this false belief, and instead celebrate this very important and sacred part of who I am. I realized after some time, that perhaps there was something inside of them that they were not comfortable with and instead criticized me. Both the masculine and feminine are to be honored. I hope that you choose to honor both too my beautiful "Queen," enjoying their expression and divine dance together.

I also have one more important thing to share...if you are wanting to attract a masculine man into your life, then you will have to get into your feminine for parts of your day because a masculine man is attracted to a feminine woman, one who takes good care of herself, has her own interests and knows how to receive. Several men I spoke to, stated that they felt confused while dating women because they experienced many to have a hard time receiving (even to have their door opened for them for example), and this turned them off. I had no idea how important and attractive it was for some men (those who were in their masculine for most of the time), just being in my feminine, until I was told by several that my energy feels very "feminine" to them. I learned later on that men are attracted to a woman's energy and it is the feminine energy that they were feeling from me and attracted to, even before meeting in person sometimes. You may find that as you declutter, not only will a more beautiful living space become your reality, you may also attract a powerfully masculine divine being to you!

If you are already in a relationship and want to feel the polarity created in a more powerful way between the masculine and feminine, then experiment with being in your feminine more. You may then feel a magical shift happen between the two of you without saying a word to your partner! You may see that as you flow into your feminine, your partner will naturally move more into their masculine. Give your partner this gift.

Your Radiant Transformation

Your feminine energy will be a powerful force as you declutter because it is one of flow. This energy is ever changing and moving and will drive you to make changes as you remove all that does not serve you in your life. Your feminine power is the force of transformation, and I will help show you how to stay in your feminine so that you are able to use this force to transform your inner and outer home. Also, when feeling overworked, burned out, exhausted or fragmented, you need your feminine energy to restore, enliven, inspire, fill you up and make you sparkle from the inside out.

Below are some of my suggestions for you to start with, to help you wake up to your magnetic feminine radiance and your inner "Queen." It is important for your decluttering journey with me that you get into your feminine as much as possible before tackling an area in your home to declutter. I feel that it will make the process more fun and relaxing for you. You may want to try one idea over the first week and see how it feels, then experiment with something else on the list the following week, etc. I am hoping that these suggestions not only help you get into your best energy to face and take action with your clutter, but help you to feel better than you have ever felt in a very long time!

Breathe In Love

I feel this is the most important thing to practice regularly so I have put it first. Find a quiet space, relax your body in any position you like, close your eyes and connect to your heart by placing your hand or fingers over it in any way that feels best to you. Open yourself up to breathe in love from your heart along with the light and love of the supportive Universe. Connect to things that bring you feelings of love, compassion and gratitude as you do this. Breathe in slowly and deeply, feeling your abdomen rise up as you inhale. Feel yourself "receiving" each breath as you connect to the love inside of your heart.

Let this be your first exercise to practice the art of receiving and connecting to your heart space...to self-love, compassion and feeling thankful. Your heart has its own mind. You will probably begin to feel safe as you melt into this space. The first time you do this heart connection you may have the urge to cry, as you realize you may have been neglecting your beautiful sacred space and your truth. Let it all out. Let this also be your first experience to "just be."

To take this exercise a little further, you can extend your feelings of love, compassion and gratitude to radiate out into your home, accepting it to be perfect just as it is today. You can also radiate your feelings out to reach all others in your life.

You will see that I provide many affirmations throughout my book. It is most effective to recite them when your awareness is in your heart. The word "art" is in "heart" which gives me the message that you become an artist and co-creator with the Universe when you connect to and act from this space. Become the artist of your own life!

Slide Those Pants Off

Take off your pants and walk around your home in your panties for a while. If you feel "boxed in," too structured or tight in your body in the moment, let it all go as you slide off your pants and slip into your feminine. As you walk around your home in your sexy and pretty intimate things, embody your feminine flowing essence, connect with how you want to feel flow in your home, and how you want to live your life free of restrictions. Feel your soft bare skin kiss the air with every glorious step you take.

Dance

Feminine energy is one of movement, so to activate this I suggest you dance. Don't just stand at the sink washing your dishes...turn on the music and move your body! One of my most recent favorite things to do with my daughters is to dance while dinner is cooking and then again as part of bedtime routine. Dancing can help raise your vibration back up to its natural "feeling good" place very quickly which can also help bring new opportunities to you.

I believe that dancing helped draw the gentleman I mentioned earlier to me, because he came into my life just weeks after I stepped up the amount of dancing I was doing at home. Something else interesting, is that this incredible gentleman told me that two weeks before he found me, he had a strong desire to learn how to dance. He felt it would be something important to know once we'd come together; so he hired a private dance instructor and started lessons. Everyone and everything is connected...so no excuses, turn on that music and dance!

Get Active

Any kind of movement is great to wake up to your feminine. Go on a walk, stretch, try yoga or another kind of exercise; and make extra trips up and down your flights of stairs at home to put things away, instead of leaving things where they don't belong, creating more clutter.

Receive Acts Of Pleasure

Feminine energy is receptive energy that opens, while masculine energy is a penetrating one. To remember this you can think of sex. It is my great hope for you that you become comfortable with believing and feeling that you deserve and can stay open to receiving all that you want in your life. In order to receive a clutter-less life you must be open to allowing this in. By doing things that feel pleasurable to you as a woman, you will be practicing the art of giving to yourself and receiving, and this will serve you in so many wonderful ways.

Below are a few examples of how you can give to yourself. Allow yourself to receive everything without thoughts or guilty feelings of what it may cost, the time it is taking up or what others may think. Replace these thoughts with this mantra, "I am open to receiving all that feels beautiful, healthy and pleasurable to my body, heart and spirit." Really try to connect with how you feel as you receive each act of pleasure.

- buy yourself a gorgeous bouquet of flowers
- get your hair done at the salon
- purchase a new sexy piece of lingerie and/or outfit
- enjoy trying on jewelry and then purchase your favorite piece
- relax as you are given a manicure and pedicure
- receive a full body massage
- take a hot bath in candlelight
- buy new make-up for a fresh look including red lipstick

- apply moisturizer all over your body slowly, loving and appreciating every part of you
- apply perfume, and every time to different parts of your body you love
- be served a delicious meal and eat slowly, as you take in the wonderful aromas and flavors

Put Your Pretty Shoes On And Swing Those Sexy Hips

There's something that sparks your most feminine flare when you slip into a fancy pair of comfortable, pretty and sexy heels, slippers or flats. Try walking around your home in your favorite pair and see what it does for you! With each step, feel the movement of your hips, and connect this sensual flow to the beauty of the oh so flowing feminine energy you radiate. As you walk around this way, feel yourself walking into your feminine, and loving yourself in these shoes. Then put some things away that you just happen to stroll by.

Receive While Leaning Back And Be A Butterfly

Next time you sit down to do a task such as write a check, answer the phone, respond to an email, or look for something on the internet, observe how you are sitting. Are you feeling tense? Are you leaning forward in your chair? Is your posture hunched over as you are writing or typing? Are you not filling your lungs fully as you inhale, experiencing shallow breathing? If you answer "yes" to any of these questions then you are most likely in your "action" mode which is being in your masculine.

In order to make the shift to your feminine (if you are not feeling comfortable with how your body feels in that moment) as you are still trying to get your tasks done, sit back in your chair and become open to receiving. Open your chest area as you straighten your posture, lean back in your chair and belly breathe. Feel the difference in your body and energy sitting this way. Put your feet on the ground and feel the support and energy from the earth move through you, and relax your body.

Complete what you were working on in a slower paced way, feeling that all you need will be provided to you. You do not need to lean forward in order to "get" what you want done or accomplished or to receive answers. Instead, lean back and be in the energy of "receiving." Feel yourself as "Queen" sitting back in your royal throne, doing things gracefully, confidently and with ease. You need to be in your masculine to get tasks done, like for business for example; just become more soft as you do things, if you feel tension in your body. Think of how you are "being" as you are "doing."

I have an interesting story...as I was thinking of ideas for my book cover, I came across a picture that showed up on my computer one day that I thought would be perfect to use. I saved that image and thought that it would save with a link of where it came from, which I did not even look at as I saved it. When I sent my lovely book cover designer the image,

I thought that I had sent her everything she needed in order for her to see if I could legally use that photo. She then told me that for some reason the link to the source of the picture was blank and therefore she could not continue with the designing, and I'd have to find another picture to use in its place. I was upset when she told me that, and then tried my best to locate that image through Google; however, it never showed up.

All of a sudden, I felt my body become stiff as it moved closer into the screen, and my chest tightened up as I tried to figure out what to do next. I then stopped myself, took a slow breath in, opened my heart centre, leaned back, relaxed my body and reminded myself of my crown. I then asked the Universe to help me as I stay relaxed, and bring to me the source of the picture. I felt confident that I would receive and just listened in for what to do.

My inner "Queen" told me to try to just do a search for "standing mirrors," and so I did this. Several showed up that looked similar to the mirror in my picture. I wrote down some link names and after looking at about four photos of different kinds of furniture, I decided to send an email to one store just to see if the picture was theirs. I felt I had to start somewhere. The store was located in the UK and at the time I sent my note, it was almost midnight their time on a Friday so I wasn't even expecting to receive a message back until at least the next day.

As I finished sending the note and taking another deep breath in, I heard my email notification sound and so I looked up. It was an email from the store! The picture did belong to that business and I received permission to use it! A few moments later I received a second email from another person there who expressed the same thing! I am very thankful I received permission, and happy I remembered to "lean back." While you are on your feet clearing physical clutter and also when speaking with someone who is in front of you, notice if you feel tight in your body or if you are standing a little forward. If you are, then take a slow deep breath, feel your body relax on the exhale and lean back more, perhaps taking a step back. Try to stay aware with how your body feels as you go about your day and as you declutter. Feel yourself receive the moment and whoever is in front of you in a peaceful open-hearted and relaxed way. Imagine flowing with "what is," yet still feeling strong in your core and grounded as you see your feet as roots going into the earth. To help remember this, you may enjoy visualizing yourself to be a beautiful tall plant at the bottom of the ocean floor. Feel yourself swaying gently and peacefully in your power with every movement of the water, with your roots secured safely in the ground.

Something else that I love imagining in those moments when I feel I have the urge to figure things out in order to make something happen, yet know it is probably best not to take action that moment, is to feel myself as a butterfly and flying away. I love butterflies because of their beauty and all of their symbolic meanings. When I feel stress in my body from too much thinking, I spread my wings and fly over to my favorite location to rest. I release myself from the energy of that place of control as I fly away. I allow all thoughts that were making me feel stressed to go from me as I travel. When I arrive at my sacred place, I feel myself landing and sinking into an energy that feels so good as I lie down in my quiet space. I allow myself to just breathe and be. I remember that this is a divine way to take care of myself in moments where I know it is best to let go of control, and instead, stay open to allowing the Universe to do for me.

Imagine the most perfect and peaceful location that feels safe; and remember to fly there and rest when needed. For example, you may enjoy resting on a large soft fluffy pillow on a small island in the middle of the ocean or under a beautiful fully grown tree in a field of flowers. Allow for the best things, people, experiences in life, and all answers to come to you. You just take care of your gorgeous sacred self in your most peaceful sacred space for the moment, and rest.

Spend Time With Your Body

I know it is strange to discuss something like this in a book on decluttering; however, I will! You will connect to your feminine as you take time to be with your body, because being in your feminine means you are in your body. Get naked on your bed to sensually and slowly touch and love every part of you. Discover what feels good as you explore your beautiful self and begin to appreciate and love all of you, including the parts of you that you wish were different looking or feeling. Really sink into this divine experience. You can bring yourself to orgasm if you wish; however, do not feel that you must, or that it has to be a goal of being with your body. If you make orgasm to be a goal, then you are in your masculine. If you just allow yourself to enjoy and stay present experiencing the moment, then you are in your feminine. Let go of all expectations.

You may want to use your favorite moisturizer or massage oil, and play music that inspires you to be in your most sensual energy as you do this. If you do happen to bring yourself to orgasm, you may find that afterward, you will feel more creative, intuitive, relaxed and connected to all of who you are; and the good news is that you do not need a partner to experience this! Learn to give to yourself first, and receive this wonderful pleasure. Bring yourself to your own state of ecstasy. You will then be prepared to share all you have in relationship. The other benefit of spending time with your body, is that you will be able to express to your partner what it is that you really enjoy.

While on the topic of giving loving attention to your body including your yoni (which is the Sanskrit term for vagina), you may want to experience breathing in life force energy from this sacred space. Receive the breath from here as you open your beautiful flower and bring your breath right up through the top of your head. Then allow the energy to flow back down through your body. Feel every part of you sparkle as you do this. Try receiving the breath through your yoni as you declutter areas of your home. This may help you to stay relaxed and connected to how sacred you are, as you create sacred beautiful clutter-free spaces in each room.

Allow life force energy to move through you, and feel this force help you move out some clutter.

Play With Your Voice

As I am trained as a speech-language pathologist, I feel I have to speak about the voice! Just as the feminine is ever flowing and changing, you can allow your voice to celebrate this too. Practice varying your pitch and intonation and see if you feel more in your feminine or masculine as you try different voices. You may also want to try slowing down your speech. Imagine feeling grounded, connected to the earth below and powerful inside; yet sensing a softness on the outside as you speak in a way that feels more gentle and at a slower rate. Try humming or singing along with your favorite tunes to connect with your feminine. You can also play with your voice to express how much pleasure you feel as you spend time with your body (as described in the previous section).

Drop To The Floor

When you are in your feminine, you are connected to your emotions. Make sure you take time to just "feel" each day, and express whatever it is that you are feeling in the moment. You want your body to be free of tightness and tension that you may be experiencing from holding back what you truly feel inside. Submit to feeling and expressing all of your emotions (this is not being in the energy of a "drama queen" by the way, which may not serve you well). You may even find that when you feel totally overwhelmed, scared or upset, that you want to drop to the floor. I still remember the moment that I naturally fell to the floor many years ago, at what I felt was the most difficult time in my life. I was totally overwhelmed, sad, confused, angry and scared. I must have felt so heavy from the weight of it all that I just fell, not being able to carry it, or be in control any longer. I remember feeling relief as I dropped down and cried. I then began to pray, which just seemed to happen naturally after the crying. I surrendered. I felt a huge weight being lifted off of me as I dropped down, expressed, felt in my body where the emotion was sitting, let it all go and asked for help. I released everything that was inside, all the clutter.

Stay on your knees or just resting on the floor until you feel you've released everything. When you feel emptied out, more at peace and like you have nothing left to do being down there, then get your beautiful sacred self up and do something that feels really good and healthy for you.

Sleep Naked

Before you go to sleep remove all of your clothes, put them where they belong and then get between the sheets naked. Think of the different masks you may have worn in the day that covered up the authentic you. Remove your masks along with your clothing and allow your bed to receive the true you.

Have Girls Only And Social Time

One way the feminine connects is through communication. Enjoy time with your female friends in person, on the phone and through the internet. You may find that when with your closest girlfriends you can easily let go and express yourself without feeling like you have to become someone else in order to "fit in." Then extend your time to be with all others you care about in your life. Use this time to practice staying present, being a good listener, and to share something about yourself.

Spend Time In Nature

The feminine is life force energy. Places like forests, mountains, parks, the ocean and lakes are abundant in natural feminine energy, so it is a good idea to spend regular time in these environments and especially when you need some rejuvenating. Take your shoes off and go barefoot to connect with the earth. Be present. Just "be." Listen to the sounds of nature. Sit on the grass, appreciating the beauty and growth of the plants and trees around you as you also connect to your inner beauty and growth.

Give All Your Senses A Treat

While the masculine loves to be in the mind in thought, the feminine loves to be in the body experiencing all of the senses. Take time to go to a market to take in the wonderful aromas and beauty of what is in front of you. Treat yourself to your favorite foods, wine tastings and decadent chocolate treats. Browse through clothing shops and touch those fabrics you are attracted to. Try on a selection of clothing including silky lingerie to experience what different fabrics feel like on your skin. Take in the scents of natural essential oils, scented candles, creams and soaps, and learn which aromas you like the best. Look through home décor stores to see interesting decorative items, and to get you excited about getting your clutter out and creating your home just the way you envision it to be.

Stand With Softness And Expose Your Palms

Remember that there is strength in softness. Also remember that feminine energy is receptive that opens. When you are feeling any sort of tension in your body, trying to control a situation or feel like you are speaking too much to the person in front of you without listening, try to allow the tension to go and relax. Imagine youself as a graceful ballerina and stand in 4th position. To find the position, begin by placing your feet in 3rd position (the heel of your front foot should be touching the area of the arch of your back foot) and then slide your front foot directly out in front of you and stop when the distance between your feet is equal to about one foot's length. Relax your body and lean it a little back. As you do this, open your hands and face your palms out as they rest at your sides. Feel the tension this time leaving through your fingertips, feel your heart opening too, breathe and let it all go. Feel yourself becoming soft on the outside yet still strong in your core, with your feet rooted into the ground. See how this affects how you communicate to others. You may feel that you want to slow down your rate of speech and speak in a softer tone as you stand this way too and with your hands relaxed. You may or may not have someone in front of you as you do this pose. You may just find it really relaxing to do as you are silent in a room by yourself in order to shift your energy. Letting go, feeling this happen through your hands, and trusting that it is ok to let go feels so good.

You can only receive something new in your hands when they are empty. While decluttering, as you put things into your hands that you will be getting rid, remember to relax and open them to expose your palms as each item leaves them and goes into the "letting go" or garbage pile. Exposing your palms each time you release something, and even doing a graceful movement with your arms may shift you into the energy of feeling soft, confident, ready and excited to receive something wonderful and new. While decluttering and getting rid of things, feel your inner masculine doing the physical sorting, picking up of objects and carrying of them, and your inner feminine feeling the pleasure in the "letting go" of the objects as they leave your hands. You may even enjoy walking around your home and also resting with your palms open and exposed to keep you connected to your feminine, and to show the Universe that you have surrendered and are ready to receive.

Be Creative

Feminine energy is the creative force. Do something that you love to do, or try something new with your hands. It does not matter how well you can do something, or how something turns out. What matters is that you just create and play! Some things you may enjoy doing are painting, sculpting, doodling, planting a garden, beading a piece of jewelry, baking, playing an instrument, sewing, writing or making a craft. One of my favorite creative things I do that makes me feel so relaxed is to bead gemstone jewelry. This hobby lead to creating a little beaded gemstone jewellery business and then having inspirational jewellery making experiences become part of my Divine Decluttering services. You can learn more about this sacred, creative and powerful experience done in person or virtually, by visiting my website. You may discover a talent you never knew you had, or find your passion or calling as you become creative too!

I am going to give you your first creative exercise to do right now. All you need is a piece of paper and your favorite writing instrument. There is also space for you to do this exercise in my free workbook that you can download at www.divinedeclutteringbook.com. This is something I want you to do, in order to honor your feminine and self-love as you think of your name. Write your first name down the left side of the page, placing only one letter on each line. You are going to use each letter of your name and think of words that are related to loving yourself and being in your feminine. At times when you are feeling sad, angry, stressed, confused, tight in your body or scared, you can think of your name and what you wrote beside each letter to try to take care of you in that moment. Below is an example of what I mean, using the English translation of my name which is "Beloved." You may even want to use this name too along with your name (i.e. "Beloved (your name)"), as you are "the beloved," and to remember to "be loved" by your own self.

Say to yourself or out loud, *I AM...*

Breathing and just "being"
Expressing
Loving myself, leaning back and letting go
Opening my heart
Vulnerable and authentic
Expanding in my flexibility, fearlessness and fun
Dreaming big, Divinely guided and supported

After completing this creative exercise and before moving on to the next section, use your workbook to write down what new things you will try, in order to connect to your feminine.

Your Life In Pictures

It is a wonderful feeling to have the vision of what you want for yourself present in your days, and especially on those days where you are feeling anything but good. You are going to create a book of pictures to represent everything that you put on your wish list, and more that you want to create for yourself in the next year or two. You will now have a way to connect with your wishes and dreams any time that you want, as you hold your book in your hand, no matter where you are and at any time of day. This will be your way to connect to your "new story." This will be your sacred and divine "My Life In Pictures" book.

My inexpensive suggestion is that you visit your local dollar store and purchase a thin binder that feels good in your hands along with binder plastic page protectors. These pages come in packages of at least ten, so they are an inexpensive investment. You will slip into each page protector one or two pictures that represent something on your wish list. You can use photographs, printouts, pictures from magazines, your own drawings, words to represent what you want, etc. There are no rules or right or wrong way to do this, just have fun!

You may want to ask me at this point why I am not suggesting creating a vision board, which is something that seems to have become so popular these days. My answer is that I tried a vision board and did not find it very effective for me. It may work for you and it is wonderful if it does. You may choose to create a vision board instead or in addition to creating a book! My experience was that while trying to focus on one picture on my board, I often became distracted with another picture that was in my line of vision. This affected my ability to deeply dive into thought and get into the visualizations and emotions connected with the one image I wanted to give some love and attention to.

The other thing that I noticed was that I was not feeling comfortable having a "display" of my dreams and wishes that could be seen by others should they walk into the room where I had it up. It was my private journey. A book will give you more privacy to collect images that are for your eyes only. When I travelled I found it frustrating that I did not have the board with me. It was too big to pack. A book can easily be put into a bag and travel with you everywhere you go. If you do use a vision board, then consider taking a photo of it with your phone so that you have it to look at when you go away.

Below are some picture ideas you may want to include in your book of dreams and wishes:

- different rooms in homes that you want your rooms to look similar to once the clutter is out
- a pretty desk area
- beautiful bed and night stands
- master bedroom closet space
- an organized arrangement you like for your make-up
- kitchen pantry with items arranged beautifully
- images of loving couples to represent whatever it is you desire in relationship such as emotional connection, more intimacy, going on picnics, travel, romance, creating together, etc. (even if you are already in relationship you can have pictures in order to help manifest what you feel is missing, into to the relationship)
- airplane en route to represent the travelling you want to do

- destinations you want to travel to
- logo from the company you want to work at
- the book cover of your upcoming book (which you can design on your own or even order a mock cover image inexpensively online)
- the body shape you imagine having (you can put a picture of your face over the one in the image to make it feel even more real)

There are so many possibilities; just connect with what you truly want and enjoy this activity! There is space in my free workbook that you can download at www.divinedeclutteringbook.com for you to write a list of the types of pictures you want to include in your book.

Having a regular routine is important in order to make progress and in order to have what you want to manifest. The most successful people in this world became successful partly because of their routine. It takes discipline to keep one and looking at your pictures may become a very important part of it, and so delightful to do! Routine practice is a more masculine energy and so you may feel that the structure of routine puts you in your masculine. This is good though because for parts of your day you will need to be in your masculine. Once you connect with your pictures, you will most likely feel yourself gracefully slide into your feminine. I hope you enjoy the expression of both energies as you move through your decluttering journey! I also hope you begin to understand the importance of both your inner masculine and feminine and how they can serve you in the best ways possible to live as the most radiant "Queen," fully connected to all the different flavors of you.

Part of my morning routine usually includes spending time looking in my book. I like the feelings that each picture brings out in me; and I enjoy carrying the wonderful feelings with me all day. Choose the time of day that works best for you to be with your pictures, and make the commitment to practice this daily if you find you like doing this. Do what feels good. All you need to do is keep listening in to your inner "Queen" and use her as your guide. You may want to begin with a small number of pictures and add more as you go along and feel the desire to. You can also choose to focus on just a few pictures at each sitting at a time. Do what feels best in the moment and remember that the more attention and focus you give to something, the more powerfully that energy expands. Since you can take the book anywhere (such as to work, appointments or your children's after school programs for example) you can also get in some extra time with your pictures in the middle of your day. You will also enjoy looking through your pictures when feeling down in order to help shift your focus to get you to a better feeling place. I have very interesting stories of how the visualizations I created with the pictures I had been looking at over several months had come to be my reality. It truly is amazing! This is also interesting...the gentleman who appeared in my life most recently, sent me a couple pictures that he said are his favorite, and they were the exact ones in my collection!

In order to get the most out of your experience with your pictures each day, I recommended you do the following. It is best to spend time looking at your images when very relaxed which is in the alpha state. The alpha state is a state between being awake and asleep and provides a bridge to the subconscious mind. When you are in this state you increase your creative energy, you can be very insightful, are more open to suggestion (which is important when wanting to self-reprogram and for self-improvement) and can visualize extremely well, all of which will help to manifest what you want in a powerful way.

There are several different ways that you can get into the alpha state, including through meditation. When you feel that you are in that state feeling so relaxed, you are ready to look at your pictures. Open your eyes and see yourself walk into the image and connect with the emotions of how you feel as you are there, and feel with all of your senses. What does it feel like, taste like, smell like and sound like? What are you doing? What are you wearing? You may find it easier to connect with all your senses with your eyes closed. You can look at the picture for a few seconds and then close your eyes and imagine the image on a large screen in front of you. Make the picture come to life in your mind's eye. Give it a heartbeat, give it energy. I will talk a little more about giving your picture a heartbeat later on. You will attract to you things that match how you feel, so make sure that you stay connected to the best feelings as you spend time with your pictures.

I have one final suggestion...if you have the wish to create something in your life that involves a particular person and imagine this person in some of your pictures (such as wanting that person to hire you for a job in their company, or be in relationship with you, or sell you their home for example), you must take care of your thoughts. I feel it is best to only focus on your own self and the emotions you feel as you connect to what you want. I would leave the face of the other person in your visualization as anonymous and allow the Universe to figure out how things will happen and who it will happen with.

You may not know what is the very best for you no matter how much you want a particular person to be part of your life experience, so it is important to leave yourself open to all possibilities instead of limiting yourself to one person. Most importantly though, I feel that it is stepping over your boundary and not allowing the freedom of choice for the person you are hoping will do or be something for you, if you focus on what you want for yourself with that person. How do you know that what you want is also best for them (especially if you have not discussed this between the two of you)? You don't and therefore, it is most important to let go of control of others energetically. Release them. Stay focused on you and on the beautiful powerful feelings you create in yourself in the scenarios you wish for, and let go of the rest.

If you are skeptical about my suggestion then do the following. Check in with your body and see how you feel as you hold on to the thought of something specific that you want with a specific person, when you don't know if that person wants what you do. Then let go of imagining that person and put an anonymous face in their place, and see how your body feels. At first, you may feel a little scared to "let go"; however, I hope that as you practice this, you experience a sense of ease, respect, peace and trust.

You will receive exactly what you wish for that is in alignment with the feelings you have been radiating outward and in the best possible way; just keep letting go of control, allow others to be, stay focused on yourself, relax, allow and deeply feel. Also, if you are a feminine woman and you are imagining being in a relationship with a masculine partner, then why not allow them the gift of being fully in their masculine as you feel them "taking" you, instead of you "taking" them and holding onto them in your mind; so let go and just stay connected to your own feelings as you feel yourself being taken by the one you desire. Create a powerful magnetic attraction and feel how your heart and spirit shimmer with excitement as you do.

I remembered the importance of dreaming and visualizing one day, as I thought about my late grandfather (my father's dad). He told me that he imagined the woman he would be married to in great detail, including what she would be wearing the first time he saw her. He used to dream about her. Then one day, he was at the park in front of his apartment building and knew that the girl he noticed sitting on the bench was "the one." She showed up exactly as he imagined her to be, even wearing the same blouse and skirt that he saw on her in his dreams. They got married and had the most beautiful life together.

I am a dreamer...I dream, create intentions, imagine, feel, let go of control and trust. I feel the unconditional love in my heart and detachment to things and others in my mind. I know you will enjoy practicing this too, and hope you also remember the concept of letting go with love as you detach from and let go of the physical clutter in your home.

You may be wondering at this point how much use this new "My Life In Pictures" book will be to you when it comes to getting rid of your clutter. You may also be asking yourself if you can get away with not creating a beautiful collection of pictures, making excuses that you don't have the time to do this and still get your clutter out in a pain-free and graceful way. To find out the answers, I suggest you take a sexy step forward into the next chapter...

CHAPTER 4
You Will Ask Yourself The Grand Question

The Grand Question

As you know, it can become very confusing and stressful to look at all of your personal possessions to try to figure out what you should keep and what you should give away. This is especially so, for when you feel many items you own are still in great condition yet you don't use them regularly, or they are just sitting around taking up space like a decorative piece that no longer lights you up like it used to yet still looks nice in the space. You may start to come up with many questions to try to figure out what to keep and what to let go of. This may keep you in a state of feeling overwhelm and fear and delay getting things done as you juggle through your answers to each question, still trying to figure out if the object needs to be released.

You my "Queen," will not have to worry about going through this exhausting list of questions because I will teach you a very simple method that will allow you to easily decide what to keep and what to let go of. You are going to feel yourself in your most powerful feminine energy with your beautiful "My Life In Pictures" book next to you, and ask yourself one question as you are trying to make the decision to keep whatever it is that is in front of you.

The Grand Question:

"*Do I want this item to show up in my book?*"

To clarify, if a snapshot of that item was featured on its own page in your book or showed up as part of a picture you already have in there (e.g. you are looking at a picture in your book of a couple kissing on the beach and your dress that you are considering getting rid of is on the woman in the picture that is to represent you), would you really enjoy looking at that page? If you feel the item is in alignment with what you want for yourself and you feel really good imagining the object in your book, then you will keep it, as long as you have a space assigned for it and you will use it. Otherwise, you will let it go.

This strategy to help remove clutter will keep you connected to your dreams and desires. If you truly want what is in your book to become your reality and what you have tried in the past has not worked for you, then it is time to try this. The more you keep focused on your wishes by feeling them as your reality, instead of feeling like they haven't come true yet, the more power you give to them. Add to this power by giving the energy of your wishes the gift of being surrounded by things in your home that align with them.

If you are stuck on deciding what to do with something that you received as a gift from a relative, friend, co-worker or someone else close to you because feelings of guilt emerge with the thought of letting it go, then let go of the guilt. Realize that the object is just that...an object. You are connected to the person that gave you this gift and will continue to show appreciation for their kind gift, no matter if it is still in your home or not. Someone in this world is waiting for that item you no longer need or use, so think about donating it or giving it to someone you know who would appreciate it.

You can also take pictures of the objects that have meaning for you (whether it is a gift from someone or something you've kept from your past as part of your memorabilia yet have no use for these items and no room for them) before giving them away, and save them in a folder on your computer with a title such as "Divine Items From My Past." If you really want to get creative, you can create a book on your computer with the photos and add a little story under each one; or print out the photos and put them in an album. You can add pictures to your online collection or physical album you create for the rest of your life without taking up valuable space in your home!

I worked with one lovely client who requested I help declutter her living and dining room space only, in order for her to feel comfortable having clients come to her home for her business. She had large amounts of clutter throughout her living space and expressed to me that so much of what she had was not hers. She inherited many items from her parents after they passed on that she had no room for, so everything stayed in boxes. She also had a collection of things from relatives that she had no use for.

There were boxes stored in her basement and attic that she never touched and every shelf and cupboard in her home was filled. I tried to encourage her to do some decluttering with me little by little in the rest of her home and not just in the area for business; however, she stated that she was not ready to do any more. She had been living with that clutter for years and years and there was no way that she could possibly keep up with the regular cleaning or even reach certain areas because of all the stuff.

About three years after I helped her in the main area of her home, this beautiful woman let me know that she had to immediately move out because of bugs...all kinds of bugs that covered every part of her home and some had wings so she got bitten throughout the nights. As she did not know how long it would take for her home to be sprayed and cleared of the intruders, she could not commit to a long term place to rent and moved from hotel to hotel and then from one rental to the next for about one year. She had to have her home sprayed several times to get rid of the bugs and decided that she would not move back and sell it instead. Now she had a huge job. She had to go through all the clutter in her home, and in a limited amount of time so that she could get it sold. If it was decluttered years before, even a little at a time, she would have saved herself a lot of stress and emotional trauma. Letting go of things from parents and the past can be very difficult. Add the stress of being invaded by bugs and it is even harder.

If after answering the one question *"Do I want this item to show up in my book?"* you begin to feel a little unsure of your answer, you can do the following. Remove the item from its location (I suggest to put it in a bag in another room), take a few slow deep breaths in as you fill up with love, then walk back in to the location where the item originally was. Take notice of how you feel. Hopefully you feel really good and some relief. Next, retrieve the object from the bag and put it back in the place you took it from. Walk out of the room then come back in and see how your feelings have changed. If your emotions shift into a place of feeling confusion, frustration, sadness, anger or worry as you look at the item visiting its old home, then you will know that your initial inspiration to remove the object to start with was your truth. You can then go ahead and remove it for good. Remember also, that the more open spaces you create in your home and inside of you, the more space you allow for new and much better things to enter your life.

I understand that we are each unique and it is not possible that only one technique for removing clutter will work for everyone and so that is why I have provided further suggestions if you find that my first one, using "The Grand Question" does not work for you. I appreciate the abundance of books on the market with such a variety of strategies to help with clutter issues because everyone will resonate with something different. I am going to offer two more strategies to help you and that will keep you connected to your heart and body, so you have a selection to choose from as you take action.

You can use your muscles because your muscles know the answers when you don't. Your body is part of nature and connected to the energy of the greater whole and to your truth. Trust what your body is telling you. You bypass the ego mind when doing the activity I describe below, and become connected to your intuitive guidance (and the voice of your inner "Queen" is part of this) which is connected to the greater whole. I struggled so terribly when trying to make the decision whether or not to leave my marriage. My intellectual mind told me to stay and continue to try and make things work, even though I tried for so long doing that. This mind also tried to convince me to stay as we were planning on moving into a new beautiful home in just a few more weeks. One morning I was in our unfinished basement, sitting on the cold concrete floor cross legged ready to start to pack some boxes for our move. I came across some of my husband's memorabilia from his past and then something inside of me said grab two boxes, so I did. The next message that came to me was to label one box as his and the other as ours. I then closed my eyes and made a request to my higher mind, which I feel is connected to my heart, "Please help me make the decision." I had never done something like this before and felt that I was being guided to from within.

As I requested help, I was holding on to one of my husband's items in my hand, holding my arm up in front of me in between both boxes. I then waited quite some time for an answer, still with my eyes closed. I focused on slow relaxed breathing and the beat of my heart, as I tried as best I could to let all thoughts go. Soon my arm slowly moved to his box. For the first time in a long time, I felt that I found my intuitive supportive voice, the one that was lost in my clutter. I felt a huge relief. I also cried for a very long time. I knew that from the peace I felt in my heart and in my body after I cried, that leaving the marriage was my truth. My mind did not know this. I knew that leaving my marriage was the path I needed to take and I also learned that I was not alone in this. I had my inner voice, my inner "Queen" that was connected to universal consciousness, to the Divine, to help me through, always by my side.

If you decide to try using your muscles then I suggest taking the object that you are unsure about getting rid of in your hand, sit comfortably, and have two boxes or bags in front of you. Identify one as the "Keep It" container and the other as the "Let It Go" container. Breathe in the loving support from the Universe as you relax as much as possible, feeling every muscle in your body loosen more and more with each exhale. Put your hand on your heart and bring your awareness to that place as you let all thoughts go. Then ask the question out loud with your eyes closed as you are holding the object, "Please help me make the decision." Then wait silently staying connected to the beat of your heart and see where your arm eventually goes. The end of your arm is so close to your heart. Trust that your arm will receive your heart's guidance and move. This is a very good exercise to connect you to your higher awareness, your "Queen" power, your heart.

I am hoping that not only will this book help you to get rid of your clutter, but also help you to become more whole and connected within. The more you nurture your connection to your heart, the more you are giving yourself love. When you declutter from a place of love, you receive it back; and your home will give the love back to you in huge ways!

I have just one more suggestion. There is also something called muscle testing where you present a statement and then test your muscles to determine what your truth is. For example, your statement may be, "This (name the item) belongs in my life." Then you test your muscle strength. If your muscle goes weak, then you know the item is not in alignment with what you want. If your muscle stays strong and you have a difficult time moving the body part you are doing muscle testing on, then you know to keep the item.

You can also ask something like this: "Is it true that I should give away my (name the item)?" Ask the question without any emotions or judgments attached, then do the muscle test. If the answer is "yes," your muscles will stay strong. There is a lot of information online about muscle testing, so I will leave it to you to research on the topic if you choose to try this method.

I am also including as a bonus in my free workbook that you can download at www.divinedeclutteringbook.com, a list of questions for you to answer should you still have difficulty letting go of any of your personal possessions after trying the suggestions described here.

I sense that all of what I am proposing above feels a little out of the ordinary for you. If you want great changes in your life, then you have to do something different than what you have been doing. As you try something new, you may feel uncomfortable. Get used to feeling some discomfort! I imagine that after some time those uncomfortable feelings will go away as you see how powerfully you are manifesting better things for yourself and starting to feel better as you get the clutter out.

You are the "Queen" of your life and so powerful, you can do this! If you continue doing what you always have been, then you will create more of the same; and you will feel more of the same miserable feelings that you have been struggling with. I want you to feel as relaxed as possible while on your decluttering journey with your "Queen" self. This is a question you may be asking yourself right now, "Can I trust in this process and the Universe to provide for me?"

The Loving Answer

Albert Einstein stated, **"The most important decision we make is whether we believe we live in a friendly or hostile Universe."** If you choose to believe we live in a friendly Universe, then you will believe that you will always be provided for in all ways that are best for you, and you can trust in this process. If you choose to believe that we live in a hostile Universe, then you will feel in a state of lack, fear and mistrust. When in the energy of trusting that the Universe is a friendly one, I feel you are choosing to live through eyes of love. When in the energy of feeling a hostile Universe, I feel you are choosing to live through eyes of fear.

I realized that for many years as I become more and more unhappy in my life as the mind clutter mountain started to form from worry and stress, I was living in a state of fear. When things were at their most horrible for me, I ended up starting to completely lose trust in life and even those in my life who were closest to me. I found that when I started to trust myself again as I learned to connect and listen to my inner "Queen," I started to trust in life and others again, one small step at a time. I noticed that really good things started to happen for me when I trusted.

When I lived in fear and my thoughts were focused on things that made me feel anxious, I created experiences in my life that felt horrible and scary...and lots of both; and it took me a long time to heal from those times. I am so thankful for that moment I woke up to understand that we attract to us what we focus on. Choose to trust in life and have pleasant thoughts, and you will attract things that feel pleasant in your life.

Albert Einstein also stated, **"The significant problems we face cannot be solved at the same level of thinking we were at when we created them."** It is very likely that the way you have been thinking and making decisions that have caused your clutter to build, may be the lower level of thinking which is connected to fear. When you choose to live through eyes of love and trust, you are putting yourself on a higher level. You are living from a higher vibration, which is your natural best feeling state as you connect with love, joy and peace. This is the energy level you want to keep shifting into in order to change your life for the better. Do you feel ready to answer the question now? Are you able to trust in this process and the Universe to provide for you?

The Soothing Statements

Decluttering with the support of your divine inner "Queen's" guidance will feel soothing. By listening to the messages that come through your heart to help you declutter, I hope you will feel more confident, loved and at peace as you let go of what you no longer need. If you choose to declutter while you are still in a state of mistrust, you may experience feelings of sadness, fear, worry, confusion and disappointment along the way. When functioning from this place, you are surrendering to the critical voice in your head. It would be best for you to recognize when this voice is speaking, because it is a part of you; just not the part that wants what is best for you. This voice comes from the most scared and vulnerable part of you and needs your love; so hear and love this voice for a moment. Acknowledge it by giving it some attention like a kiss; and then tell it that you are the "Queen" and hear this part of you, yet are choosing to believe and do something else. Continue to love this part of you though. You might even imagine embracing this part in your arms to soothe her and quiet her down; then go ahead and make the shift inside to choose to surrender to the voice in your heart...to love.

Read the statements below. Then check in with your body to see how it responds, and how you feel as you read each one. The first statement in each pair can be imagined as something you would say as the critic in your mind. The second statement in each pair can be imagined as something you would say when in your heart space. You can either choose to kiss your clutter goodbye with doubt or divine trust. The choice is yours.

While decluttering I use the critical voice in my mind as my guide.
While decluttering I use my inner "Queen's" divine guidance.

I see decluttering as a reason to make others happy or to impress others.
I see the purpose of decluttering as a time for spiritual and emotional growth and to make me happy.

I declutter and end up feeling worn out and resentful.
I declutter and end up feeling happy, energized, excited and at peace.

I am decluttering without patience.
I am decluttering with patience.

I criticize and judge myself as I declutter.
I love myself as I declutter, without self-criticizing or judging.

I am attached to things.
I am attached to self-love and my inner "Queen's" divine guidance.

As I declutter I feel connected to those I live with by arguing.
As I declutter I feel connected to those I live with by loving them.

I see the purpose of decluttering as a way to get more love from someone else.
I see the purpose of decluttering as a way to deepen my own self-love.

I see having a perfect living space as more important than knowing my authentic self.
I see knowing my authentic self as more important than having a perfect living space.

I feel disappointment if there is still remaining clutter that needs attending to, that I did not get to when I thought I would.
I feel satisfied even if there is still some remaining clutter to clear, that I thought I would be able to get through.

I believe that a decluttered home will never happen.
I believe that a decluttered home is my reality.

I fear that I will need what I just gave away.
I declutter knowing that I will be provided with what I need when I need it.

I feel like a victim in my life and see clutter as something that happens to me.
I feel in control of my life and see clutter as something that I create.

I declutter in a negative frame of mind and with limited views.
I declutter with a positive frame of mind and thoughts of unlimited possibilities.

I give things away with anger, only thinking of my own personal needs.
I give things away out of generosity, and feel grateful for what I do have.

Are you ready to meet your beautiful inner "Queen?" If so, please use your arms to give yourself a big hug as you slowly take a walk to your largest mirror, or to find a hand mirror and be prepared to hold it up. When you have done this, you are ready to enter the next chapter...

CHAPTER 5
You Will Meet Your Queen In The Mirror

Mirror, Mirror On The Wall

"Mirror, mirror on the wall, who's the fairest one of all?" "Why you are my precious Queen."

I know that you may not feel this way right now and I'm absolutely sure you don't feel that your home feels this way either at this moment; however, you are going to experience a transformation. Not only will you transform what your home is going to look like and feel like, you are also going to transform how you feel about yourself. You are going to start working on this in front of your mirror. Just as you will create a living space that reflects who you are, and what you want in your life, you are going to be able to look at your reflection in the mirror and have it express back to you, the beauty of all that you are. This powerful tool will create magic in your life. Just be patient, and you will see!

I could not believe how quickly things started manifesting for me when I increased the amount of mirror work I did and in the way I was doing it, which I describe below. I have never read a book on mirror work. I just used my intuitive guidance from my inner "Queen" and trusted that this will create miracles in my life. I could feel my energy shift to a really good place as I spoke to, and also listened to my reflection. I could feel that I was bringing myself to a healthier vibration that aligned with all I wanted in my life.

For example, when I felt satisfied with the amount of clutter I had removed from my living space to prepare for the life I dreamed of having, I started increasing the amount of mirror work I did. I increased the amount as I felt my inner "Queen" guiding me to. This was the time I sensed that the gentleman I could feel inside of me, was very close to me energetically. I felt guided to bring myself to feeling my very best just for me, and was supposed to do this with the mirror.

We receive what we are, and I was ready to receive the best gentleman I could ever imagine. That meant that I needed to first become the best woman that I could imagine being for myself. He then found me, just weeks after spending more time with my reflection. Perhaps this is why. I was able to unconditionally love, accept and see all of who I am. Perhaps it is because I could, that he was also ready to see me. If you want to attract "The One," then become "The One." If you want a hero, then become one. It all starts with you.

My clients love when I teach them my recipes for a more exciting and clutter-less life. It is so wonderful to receive emails from my clients after having Skype sessions, where I teach them my techniques for manifesting. Below is an email from one of my beautiful clients who delayed contacting me for one year after our last session, where she said she would continue to follow through with her decluttering program we created together. She contacted me in a panic asking if I could meet with her that day over Skype, as she was feeling in real rough shape.

She expressed to me that she had not followed through with her decluttering over the year as she said she would, and now her health, living space and relationship was suffering horribly. She felt like she was going downhill. Her boyfriend of many years kept putting off committing to something more serious, and this made her feel even more upset and confused. I agreed to meet with her at 10pm that evening which is something I would not typically agree to do so late; however, I sensed her urgency and wanted to help in any way I could.

During our meeting I gave her some easy decluttering tasks to complete in her living space that she agreed to do, and then focused on having her practice mirror work. This is the email I received from her less than one week from the time of our late night session:

"Hi Aimee!!!!! I had an amazing weekend! He proposed to me!!!!!! ... I'm sooo excited!!! I have been doing the mirror talk, and I think it helps! ... Yayy!!!!!!"

Below is part of another email I received one day following a Skype consultation with the most wonderful and successful business woman who spent most of her days in her masculine. She felt that this was affecting her connection with men. She was wishing for a relationship, and so I helped get her started in reconnecting to her feminine in order to attract the relationship she imagined having. She also was wishing that the one man she had been involved with for many years (with no commitment as he would not commit to anything serious as he was not yet divorced) would commit to her fully, and call her, as he had been out of touch for quite a while. She also decided that if she did not hear from him again, then someone even better would show up for her. Part of the session was spent practicing powerful mirror work. This is part of her note to me after we met over Skype:

"Hi Aimee! I had a nap and went to a beautiful yoga class. I came home to meditate and do our exercises and guess who called right then wanting to come over?? I said yes, and we actually had a beautiful few hours together. Something about this feminine vulnerability and communication is affecting him. He said something like "I want to create the safe space for your heart." That's unprecedented. Whether he's "The One" or not doesn't really matter. I know now to stay focused on me and my femininity, and allow the men to respond. I so appreciate your support and guidance – thank you!"

The gentleman who came over was the one she was hoping would connect with her again, and this happened just hours after she did the exercises and mirror work we practiced together over Skype. Trust that things can happen, in an instant sometimes, when you make a powerful shift in your energy. This also very much includes how you are changing energy in your living space. Remember that everything is energy so every small thing you do to bring you to a better feeling place and into a deeper connection with your authentic self is important!

Are you also starting to understand that in order to change your life experience, YOU must change? There is no need to try to change the person that you wish would shift. All you need to do is shift what is going on inside of you, and life will reflect back to you all that you are and what you feel about yourself. My client was constantly feeling hurt by this gentleman because she was choosing to spend time with him while he was also spending time with another woman. She was choosing to be with someone who would not give himself fully to her. She was also not showing up for herself fully, because she was disrespecting what she knew she needed to feel at peace and safe in her heart. Her heart was hurting, yet she was having such a hard time letting go of him. She decided at the time that we met, that she needed to protect her heart and connect with the most sacred part of herself that she has been avoiding for so many years. She started to do this in the mirror. If you are ready to make a powerful shift happen inside of you, then keep on reading...

I suggest that you go to the mirror first thing in the morning, and again right before bed and look at your reflection as you speak. I use two kinds of mirrors to do my mirror work. One of them is large sized and on the wall. The other is a small framed mirror that I can hold. I love to wake up each morning to connect with my inner "Queen" in the large mirror, and again each night as I meet her in the small one while relaxing, before I sleep.

I enjoy speaking into a larger mirror when I want to connect with feeling more powerful in business, and as a communicator for a couple examples. You may also enjoy speaking into the mirror while relaxed in bed, in order to connect more fully to some of the more intimate aspects of your feminine you feel you need to spend more time with. Try both ways and see how each experience makes you feel. I also recommend to purchase a mirror with magnetic back (that you can easily find at a dollar store) and stick it on your fridge if it is magnetic. While waiting for your food to cook you can use that time for mirror work. If you are trying to watch what you eat, you can also look into the mirror before opening your fridge to ask your inner "Queen" if she thinks it is a good idea to put into your mouth what you are craving that moment. Then listen to what she says back to you.

You may want to write down some phrases to express to yourself in the mirror, and repeat them daily (remembering that routine and repetition is powerful); and also just express whatever comes up through your spirit in that moment. This may feel uncomfortable at first; however, I hope that this feeling changes for you and that you will eventually come to enjoy this practice so much.

In the remainder of this chapter I describe the steps you will take as you begin this sacred experience of connecting...

Look At Your Reflection In Silence

As you come to face your beautiful reflection, take slow deep breaths and just "be" in the silence. Take the time to bring your eyes up to look into them and see what comes up for you. Being in the silence can be healing itself. I remember when I did this for my first time many years ago. I could barely look into my eyes or at my face for more than a few moments. Not only did I not like looking at my skin that had a horrible rashy appearance from the stress at the end of my marriage, I felt horrible because I knew I was not living the way I imagined myself living and felt like my true self was lost...lost in my clutter.

Each day though, I forced myself to just spend a few seconds in silence looking, and eventually I broke down and cried. Crying is such a healthy release of emotions and healthy for your body, so if you feel like crying, let it all out. Get into your feminine and express. Be vulnerable; be you. As you cry, feel your inner clutter leave your body through your tears, and each time you exhale. Breathe in self-love that your inner "Queen" has for you, along with the love of the supportive Universe. You may even want to touch your reflection and also touch any part of you that you can see in the mirror, in a loving way, imagining that your inner masculine is giving to your feminine...soothing and loving her. This is a beautiful way to practice the exchange of giving and receiving within your sacred self.

Listen To Your Inner "Queen"

Once you complete the first step, choose to believe that you can have something better for yourself. Believe that your home will become your clutter-free and sacred "Queendom" that makes you feel at peace, supported, relaxed and safe. You will express statements into the mirror imagining that your inner "Queen" is the one speaking to you. She will be speaking to the part of you that still feels a little scared and unsure of the process.

Below are some examples of statements this voice wants to express to you. State as many of these as you wish and imagine your image in the mirror as your best self, the radiant "Queen." Listen to what she is telling you.

(Your name), I love you and accept all of you unconditionally.
Wouldn't it be wonderful if you could create the life of your dreams?
Wouldn't it be wonderful if you could clear out all the items in your home that you no longer need one simple step at a time?
Wouldn't it feel powerful to take inspired action?
Wouldn't it feel so supportive if you lived in a space that is in alignment with what you want and what you dream of?
Wouldn't it feel so heavenly to have your bedroom feel like your safe space, organized and romantic?
You are on your way to creating a beautiful clutter-free home.
I am helping you every step of the way.

What you do today will be perfect.

Your dreams are coming true for you or something even better.

You are the most valuable woman.

What you focus on will expand, so stay focused on thoughts that feel best to you.

You are a divinely feminine woman.

Your heart and spirit want your attention, so listen to what they express to you.

Your home is your sacred space.

You are sacred.

You have a unique gift to share with the world.

Take care of yourself first.

You are love.

Your home is supporting you in all you want.

Use my free workbook that you can download at www.divine declutteringbook.com to write down the statements you like from here and some of your own.

Express Your Response

Now that your "Queen" has spoken to you, what are you feeling? I want you to now take this time to look in the mirror and express whatever feelings come up. Connect with your emotions. Connect with the raw authentic you. Feel your inner "Queen" and the Universe/your higher power right there with you. You are not alone. You have complete support. Write down what you were feeling in my free workbook that you can download at www.divinedeclutteringbook.com.

Honor Your Self With Love

Now that you have expressed and released your emotions, you are ready to give yourself lots of loving! Look in the mirror, and with your imagined crown upon your head and hand over your heart, speak to your reflection. To make this exercise even more powerful, you may want to wear a real crown. I used one of my children's crowns for fun that came with a princess costume. Some days I even walked around my home wearing this tiara as my kids wore theirs. It was a great experience to see what feelings came up at different times when I wore it. You may want to try this too! Choose to say as many of the statements below as you wish, each time you go to the mirror.

I love all of who I am unconditionally.
I accept myself just as I am.
I am unapologetically me.
I am the Queen of my life.
I am a radiant woman.
I am valuable.
Is am worthy of love and having a home that feels like my sacred sanctuary.
I am enough.
I am so loved and so lovable.

I am the light and my radiance shines outwards.

It is good that I cry and express my feelings.

My own self-care comes first.

I love my home and accept it as it is today, just as I accept all of who I am today.

My home supports me in all I want.

My home is my "Queendom," my sacred sanctuary.

I am beautiful from the inside out.

I am a powerful creator.

I live in a clean organized space.

Today I do what I can as I listen to my body and inner voice, and that is always enough.

Everything that I take out to use, I put back.

I am creating the life of my dreams.

I am easily removing the clutter from my life.

I am becoming more clutter-free every day.

My purpose is going to show up as I begin to do more of what I love.

I am getting better and better in every way each day.

Today I am releasing some clutter from the (name the location).

Today I am doing something good for my Goddess self first, before doing for others.

I am getting the most important thing done today first.

I only bring into my home what I love and is in alignment with what I want.

I am letting go of what I do not need with ease today.

I am ok with the unknown, and living with some uncertainty of what is to come. I live feeling as good as I can each day.
I love to give away things that no longer belong in my life.
I am attracting a beautiful living space into my life that makes me feel relaxed, happy, supported, safe and at peace.
I am powerful and my dream is coming true, or something even better.
I am saying "yes" to me and all I want.

I included many "I am" statements because these two words are of great strength when used together. Anything that follows "I am" begins the creation of it. Reciting, listening to and writing "I am" statements are all very powerful exercises.

Write your own affirmations, "I am" statements and anything you like from here in my free workbook that you can download at www.divinedeclutteringbook.com.

Hear About Your New Reality

This is the most exciting part of mirror work for me and I hope it becomes this for you too! Now is the time you get to hear your sacred "Queen" talk about life, imagining that all you want has become your reality. You are meeting your "Queen" self in the future and listening to what she is experiencing. This is a powerful exercise. I feel that it will help you shift your vibration and get on the same frequency with what it is that you want as you feel yourself become excited, trusting that as you take inspired action, your dreams will become your reality. Below is an example of something you might hear your "future self" express to you.

My radiant Queen, you won't believe what you receive! Everything that you want is coming true for you or something even better! You just keep going and keep your focus on removing your clutter, one step at a time from your home, and from inside of you. Remember to stay focused on the present, feeling good with what you have in your life right now. Keep your regular routine and rituals. Trust that a beautiful clutter-less and organized home is going to be yours. You are a powerful magnificent manifestor! Take inspired action when you feel the calling to. I love you (your name). Please just keep taking your graceful steps forward, one elegant step at a time, with your crown upon your head, self-love and compassion in your heart and the biggest smile on your face. Always feel thankful. Accept how you are today, and everything as perfect...and keep going!

Use my workbook that you can download at www.divinedecluttering book.com to write down the words from your future "Queen" self.

Imagine how good you will feel once you complete your mirror work each day, and how it will drive you to get your physical clutter out! In your awakened and glowing "Queen" power, you will be ready to take action!

"Mirror, mirror on the wall, whose inner and outer home is the fairest one of all?"

What do you think your answer will be upon completing daily visits with your inner "Queen" in the mirror after some time?

You are very close to being ready to face your physical clutter in your home, to start clearing it out! There is just a little bit more you need to know first; so when ready, please take peaceful steps forward feeling your feet kissing the ground below you, into the next chapter...

CHAPTER 6
You Will Enjoy Your Heartfelt Preparations

Giving Your Home A Heartbeat

I know that you really want your dream of a decluttered life, inside and out, to manifest. It will certainly happen if you choose to take action. You are able to take action because you are alive with a strong heartbeat and can move. I want you to do something this moment that may seem a little odd to you. Remember that to get a different result than what you have received in your past, you must do something different. So here it goes...I am suggesting that if you want your decluttered dream life to come true, then give that life a heartbeat, as I briefly mentioned earlier. Make your dream come to life, picture it moving towards you as you move towards it. My intuition guided me to try this. This journey is about bringing more love through your heart into your life, isn't it? You move into your feminine when you move into your heart space. Perhaps then what I am suggesting makes sense!

This is what you can do ... Close your eyes, imagine a large white movie screen appear in front of you, and with your eyes still closed, see an image appear on that screen. Start by visualizing one room in your home in the state you wish it to be in once all the clutter is removed, and everything is neatly organized and in place. You can even imagine different décor and wall colors if these are some things you want to change, and the scents and sounds in the room along with how the objects in there feel as you touch them/use them. You may even have a picture in your new "My Life In Pictures" book to represent the room you want to have.

As you see this image come to life, visualize that it is alive with its heart beating. You may see the image expanding and contracting as if the entire room is a beating heart, or you may envision this room moving closer and closer to you as you move closer to it. The room may have its own voice and expresses to you (just think of how many television ads and children's shows you have seen where inanimate objects come to life), or you may imagine something else. The point is that you want to give your desire as much of a feeling that it is alive as possible, so that you can imagine it coming towards you as you take steps towards it.

You also can imagine that you want to become a match in frequency to what you see coming towards you. See yourself as a magnet attracting what you want. See yourself as a TV and turning to the same station as the one on your movie screen that holds the picture you've created. You are energy and your energy moves outwards as it vibrates. One of my favorite science projects I did in public school was to show patterns of different sound waves moving through sand, that filled the entire bottom of a long glass tube. It was fascinating to me as I saw the wave pattern in the sand change as the frequency of the sound I sent through one end of the tube changed. Connect with your emotions and imagine that the energy you create is helping what you want, come to be.

Are you ready to receive what you see moving closer to you? Are you ready to create beautiful spaces as part of your "Queendom?" If you are, then I know you will do everything to clear the clutter out of the way for it to come to you and be yours! Once you have practiced visualizing a room with a heartbeat, continue doing this for all of your other rooms while you are in the process of decluttering each one.

Opening Your Mail

Now that you have made your decluttered home come to life with a heartbeat, it has the ability to speak to you. This is your chance to hear from your personal space, imagining that the clutter is already out. Remember that if you do the same thing over and over you will get the same results you have gotten up until now, so perhaps you can give this a try and see your objects as alive! Even though the inanimate objects in your space cannot feel emotions as you can, they do hold energy and you can give them meaning. Everything is energy and everything has an effect on your life either consciously or subconsciously.

I want you to try to imagine how the items you choose to keep once your decluttering is done would feel, if they could speak. Imagine how they would feel, living in clean spaces that fit them, and with all the clutter removed. This may be an important exercise for you to do so that you start respecting what is in your space more than you have been in your past. As you begin to connect more fully to your beautiful feminine "Queen" energy in order to celebrate and respect all of who you are, you will find that you will become more aware of also wanting to honor and respect your living space, and everything in it...your "Queendom." Below is a sample letter that I wrote for you, with me speaking for the objects in one of your rooms that you imagined you've decluttered. You will find space in your free workbook that you can download at www.divinedeclutteringbook.com to write your own fun, creative and meaningful letter from your objects. Take the chance and try something different and do this, even if it feels strange to! Let all judgements go. Judgments come from your critical voice in the mind. Move into your heart and try this. You may want to refer to what you wrote as you begin to declutter each room.

Dear my beautiful Queen,

Thank you for doing all of the work to release the clutter from this room. You are doing an incredible job! We...meaning all the objects you chose to keep in this room including me, feel so much better now that you are getting rid of everything that has been taking up space and not being used. We are now ready to support you and all you want with zero distractions from all of the clutter that used to live on the shelves and in piles on your floor. We can finally breathe freely and look forward to seeing you happily, confidently and sensually walk across the room in your radiance, instead of watching you trip over things and sometimes

*stop to think whether or not you should clean something in here, and
then choose not to as you get busy with something else.*

*Please use all of us to help you create what you want in your life. Please
connect every object in this space with a thought that makes your heart
sing so that each time you look at each one, you can remember how we
are supporting you in your desires. For example, for the candlesticks, if
you want more romance in your life then connect to the most romantic
feelings you can as you look at them on the shelf. They will support you.
When looking at your neatly organized drawer of silverware, think of
how life is "serving" you well. Each time you place a spoon or fork of
delicious food into your mouth, remember that you are worthy of
receiving love and everything that is yummy in life.*

*When looking at your neatly hung blouses you like to wear for business,
you can connect to how they are supporting you in creating your dream
job or finding your purpose. When selecting something sexy to wear to
bed from your organized drawer that is no longer packed to the top,
connect to how this beautiful piece enjoys being on your body, feeling
your femininity. Feel yourself comfortable and confident in your skin.
And for one final example...when looking at the clock on your shelf,
remember to be in the "now" instead of thinking and worrying about
the future or choosing thoughts that don't make you feel good about
your past. Stay in the space between those two places...stay present; and
instead of staring at something in the room you know needs to be put
away or cleaned, do it that moment if it will take no longer than a couple
minutes to do!*

It costs nothing to use whatever you can in each of your rooms to support you in what you want. It may cost you everything however, if you choose not to try something different, to shift the energy in your home and inside of you, especially if you feel you are at rock bottom and have tried everything else to get the clutter out of your life. You have chosen all of us objects to stay in your home for a reason. We must look really good as you imagine us in your "My Life In Pictures" book! Thank you for giving us the opportunity to support you in your journey! What you believe is what you shall receive...believe that we can all support you to create a beautiful clutter-less and radiant life! You are sacred and the most valuable woman worthy of this!

With Love, from all of your treasured possessions in this room

I hope that this idea of how to look at the objects in your space will spark your creativity as you choose what to keep and what to let go of in order for you to receive the most benefit from each one. I remember, when I was at my lowest point, how much it meant to me when I chose to use the objects in my space this way as support, especially at a time I did not want to socialize very much, wanting space to be just with myself for a little while. With each supportive thought I chose to think while looking at each object, I could sense myself feeling better and better each day.

Only choose to keep items that you imagine you'd want showing up in your "My Life In Pictures" book and only what you have room for and will use. Allow everything in your home to serve you well! Remember too, that the more space that you create and leave open, the more room you have for new opportunities and things to come to you; so even though you may want a lot of things around you to be of support, it really is better to have less than more. Remember, this is a book about decluttering, so let lots of things go! Fill you and your space up with love, not "things!"

Thinking And Speaking Through Love

Practicing as a speech-language pathologist I analyze "utterances," and so I am quite "tuned in" to the structure of sentences that others express. While decluttering, it is important to take a look at what and how you are expressing. What thoughts are you projecting in each of your utterances? Is what you say a reflection of what you really want? How do you feel after you produce your statements related to your clutter when speaking to yourself and to others? You have a choice to either express things in a way to make you feel happy, supported and loved or express things in a way that results in you feeling down, unsupported, doubtful, anger, pressured, guilty and scared. Remember the "Soothing Statements" in Chapter 4? Below are a few more for you to read, and that I hope you find to be helpful examples as you practice letting go of what no longer belongs in your life.

The first statement in each pair can be imagined as coming from the fearful voice in the mind. This voice may not want you to have what is best for you. You may feel this in your body as you read or say each statement out loud. The second statement can be imagined as coming from the heart space, through the inner "Queen," through love. Choose to declutter with divine trust and love instead of with doubt and fear. Make sure to check in with your body to see how you feel as you read each one or state each one out loud.

I bought this life jacket because we had a boat many years ago. We sold the boat, but what if I need this life jacket for a trip in the future?
This life jacket will be of good use to someone else now. If I need one in the future, I know I will have one to wear.

I want to keep my 25 pairs of socks in case I don't have time to do the laundry.
I can give 10 pairs away because for what is important to do, I always make time for.

I have to spend time checking my e-mail first thing. What if it is urgent?
If there is something urgent I don't respond to, there are others ways to reach me.

It is important to read the paper every day.
Life will go on whether I read the paper or not, and I trust that what I need to know will be presented to me.

Listening to the news first thing makes me feel on top of things.

Having silence first thing gives me space and time to get centred in my thoughts and focused for the day.

I had a rash and needed this cream to clear it last year. What if the rash comes back?

Why should I hold on to this cream? Do I wish for another rash? I will throw it out instead.

My last boyfriend bought this bulky jewellery box for me. It is not very practical but it holds meaning for me.

I will give the jewellery box away as I want a new relationship to come into my life. I am ready now to let him go and let the box go too. The good memories are in me, not in the box.

This bin contains projects I completed at my old job. I'm in a new career now but worked so hard on all this, how can I throw it all out?

All this can go. I am letting go of my past in order to move forward in my current career. I feel confident in my decisions to change careers. My past job does not define who I am. I just "am."

I love my book collection even though I don't refer to many of them anymore. Sometimes people come over and want to borrow some. I can't give them away.

I will only keep my favorites and those that align with who I am and where I am in my life now. I will always have something on my shelf

that may be helpful to one of my guests should they ask for something good to read.

I haven't referred to any of this reference material in my filing cabinet for over three years, but "what if" I need something for a future client I see?

I can get rid of most, as there is quick and up to date information on the internet. The less clutter in my thoughts of future "what ifs," the more clear space I have in my mind.

I like to have emergency medicines and pills in my bathroom cabinet next to my toothpaste and floss so I can see where they are in case I need them.

I will store emergency medicines and pills in a bin I can easily get to however, some place out of my direct view. This way I am not thinking about these items daily because I prefer to believe that I rarely or never need them.

I lived in these two pairs of pyjamas last year when I was fighting a bad virus. I have not worn them since but they are too comfy to give up.

I will get rid of these two pairs of pyjamas. I have other ones to wear. I wore these two during an awful time that I want to forget about.

These boxes of chocolates were gifts to me a few months back. I am trying to watch my weight, but they are from close friends.

The thought is what counts so the chocolates can go. I am thinking about

my food choices. When I invite guests to my home I will buy some fresh treats.

Learning Perfectly Positive And Present Speech

Now that we are on the topic of speaking, I am going to share just a little more about it. I recommended that when you speak, you express more about what you want rather than what you don't want. We live in an attraction-based Universe so you activate energetically whatever you speak about, think, feel and believe. If your energy focus is on something that does not make you feel good as you talk about what you don't want, you may attract experiences that match that feeling. If you energy focus is on something that makes you feel good as you talk about what you want, you will attract experiences that match this feeling. That is why I suggest you focus on what feels good as you declutter and let go of thoughts, beliefs and words that do not feel good. Also, if for example you hear news about someone or something that brings on sad feelings, instead of sitting in the sadness, send out loving thoughts and energy to the person or situation you are thinking about because this will benefit both you and the receiver of the energy.

I have a story for you... when I decided to turn my gemstone jewellery making hobby into a little business, I had several shops interested to sell what I made. The first place that sold my jewellery was a posh cosmetics studio/gift boutique in midtown Toronto. This shop was in a pocket of the city that is not high traffic so the only way you would really find this studio is if you had heard about it through someone. When I started to sell to stores, I told myself that I want this hobby to be totally separate from my work as a speech pathologist and decided to not share with my colleagues that I was going to sell my designs. When I dropped off my jewellery to the studio I had in my mind that I really hoped no one from my work comes to this place, especially the head of my department, just in case she should see my collection. When I think back, I don't even know why I was worried as only my first name appeared on the jewellery tags that went with each piece; however, at that time of my life I worried about just about everything!

There really was nothing to worry about...I just wanted this creative part of me to be something I shared with others outside of my work. That was just my choice at the time. When I went back to the shop to drop something off a few days after they received their first collection from me, I was told that my first piece sold a few minutes ago. They told me that a woman who was having her hair done purchased it. I was surprised as I did not know that this cosmetics studio had a hair salon too. "Oh no" said the boutique's owner. "The hair salon is not part of my studio. It is its own business upstairs in the building. They rent space from us and use the room up there."

A few moments later the owner mentioned in passing the woman's name who bought my piece as she talked about the hair studio. Guess who it was? It was the head of my department at my job! I worried about this happening and wished she would not come in and she did, and on the same day I was there! I have no idea which part of town this lovely woman lives in and I would never expect that she would visit this little hidden place. What is the likelihood of something like that happening? Now will you believe me, and start to think, feel and talk more about what you do want instead of what you don't want?

My next suggestion is that when you declare something, that you state this not just in the future tense, but in the present. It is important to state what it is that you do want after expressing what it is that you don't want. Yet an even more powerful way to speak is to express next in the present tense. The Universe responds to what is presented to it. Therefore, it is better to think and speak in the present tense when you want to make a change, and then connect to how this feels in your body.

I remembered the importance of speaking in the present while thinking of my late grandmother (my mother's mom). She was a holocaust survivor. While on the train that was on its way to the concentration camp, there was a doctor and his family next to her. He offered my grandmother something through a needle to end the suffering right then and there, as he was going to do for the members of his family in the boxcar and himself. My grandmother's response to him was, "I am ok," and refused the offering. She was one of the most positive people I know. Perhaps she survived because of the inner shift she made to feel as best she could, no matter what was going on in the moment for her. There is no way to know for sure, yet perhaps it was because of that and having complete faith and trust, that she survived.

If you say you *will* do something, or *will* get something, it means you did not yet do it or do not yet have it. This to me makes me feel lack, and affects how I feel, and lack will likely attract more lack. If you reword your utterances into the present tense to show the Universe you are doing it or already have it, that you are abundant; and connect with the good feelings as you are in this space, you will be in the energy to attract what you want. Now is the time to believe that you can become more aware of how the words you express feel to you. Express what feels good and "fake it 'til you make it!" See if you feel the differences in your body as you use different words; I do, and that is why I like to play around with trying out different words in my thoughts and speech because I want my body to always feel good. I can only make suggestions to you based on my experiences. However, you must do what feels best for you.

Remember when I mentioned the time when I really wanted to find a job as a speech pathologist where I would not have to drive one to two hours one way, to get to clients? This is what I was doing for eighteen years up until the time I left my marriage and it totally exhausted me. At the time I felt like I could no longer imagine doing this for much longer, my intuition told me to start believing that the perfect job would show up. It expressed to me that it would show up, as long as I believed that I could have it, and as long as I took baby steps towards it when I felt my inner voice expressing me to.

I wished to be in private practice, doing contract work in schools close to home, receiving double the pay and working half the hours I had been. I felt that if I was doing that kind of work then part of my day would be open for me to pursue my other passions. I then heard of a company located close to home that hired speech therapists to do contract work in schools. This seemed ideal. However, I was too scared to make the move to enquire about the work. Having been in the same job for eighteen years made me feel "safe" I think, even though I was unhappy from the stress of all the travel I had to do each day.

I wasn't yet fully ready to leave the "safe" space of my job and take a big action step by visiting the company. Instead, I did something else. I started to tell myself that I was already in my dream job. My inner "Queen" told me to do this. I spoke out loud to myself, my friends and a counsellor I was seeing for a while who supported me through my divorce. I did not care if people thought I was nuts as I did this. I was ready to take the chance and see what would come of it. As I spoke, I really tried to believe that what I was expressing was already true. I said daily, "I am in my dream job seeing clients in schools close to home for double the pay and half the hours of my old job." I let go of figuring out how or when this would happen. I wanted the Universe to take care of that part for me.

What I was doing was fooling my subconscious mind to believe that I was already in the place I wanted to be in. Your subconscious does not know what is real and what is not, so I started to feed it everything that I wanted. Just a few months later, I decided to go to a conference for speech therapists. I thought of this as a baby step in action to move towards what I wanted, because attending conferences is something that I did not do very often. While at the event, a woman came up to me and asked if I was Aimee. I told her that I was, and then she handed me her business card. She said "call me" before walking away. I looked down at the card and she was the owner of the company I wanted to enquire about that I heard was near my home!

When I got home from the conference I immediately updated my resume from eighteen years earlier, called the woman the next day, was offered an interview, went to the interview and was hired on the spot! My pay was now double what it had been and I was working half of the time and driving shorter distances, sometimes only two blocks from home to see clients. I received exactly what I wanted. I was shocked! This happened like magic!

Getting back to the three types of statements, below are some examples of them. The first statement is written in the negative form. Check in with how you feel as you state this one. This is a good place to start as it is important to know what you don't want and connect with how you feel when in this space. Once you become aware of what you don't want and move through the emotions that you may have about this, it is best to shift your focus to what it is that you do want. This statement is the second one in each group and will probably bring you to feeling better inside, as you bring your attention to what you want, instead of what you don't want. Notice how you feel as you read each one.

The final statement in each grouping I feel is most powerful. It is stated in the present which sends the message to the Universe that what you want already exists. It is now up to you to believe that you have it already and it is already true. You have to be able to connect with what that feels like. Don't worry about figuring out how the final result will happen. Let that go. Just remember to keep listening in to your inner "Queen" for guidance. Then take inspired action when you receive the inner calling to. Even the smallest baby step is an action step.

As long as you follow what your inner "Queen" tells you to do as you declutter, and take inspired action, you will make progress in your goal. As you enter each room and with your crown upon your head, I want you to state what it is you want, as if it already exists. For example, if you are ready to tackle your bedroom closet you might say the following before beginning to sort: "My closet holds only the clothes that I feel best in." "I love looking at everything in my closet." "The outfits that I love to wear to feel sexy are lined up on this side."

Read each statement below and take note of how you feel in your body as you recite each one. There is room for you to write your own in your free workbook that you can download at www.divine declutteringbook.com.

I don't want a messy kitchen.
I want a clean kitchen.
I have a clean kitchen.

129

I don't need thirty pairs of socks.
I will keep only ten pairs of socks.
I have only ten pairs of socks.

I don't want crumbs on my bed.
I want to keep my bed clean. I will only eat in the kitchen.
I have a clean bed because I only eat in the kitchen.

I will not check my emails every few minutes.
I will schedule time to check my emails twice a day.
I check my emails twice a day.

I don't want a job that leaves me feeling drained at the end of each day.
I want to be doing something that is in alignment with my soul's calling
and leaves me feeling inspired and happy at the end of each day.
I am doing something that is in alignment with my soul's calling and
leaves me feeling inspired and happy at the end of each day.

Now that you have practiced expressing in a different way, I will give you a break from speaking as you quietly read about what you can do to release the clutter from your mind. When you are ready, please bring your gorgeous goddess self into the next chapter...

CHAPTER 7
You Will Elegantly Follow These 12 Practices To Clear Your Mind

People seem to be busier than ever these days. Our minds may be cluttered with schedules that have become completely full leaving little to no room to be spontaneous or to rest, long to-do lists, thoughts of other people's problems, our own problems, our past experiences, fears and worries about our future. Having a cluttered mind can result in forgetting what needs to be done and forgetting where things are (so you may decide to leave all things out in the open to make your hunt through your clutter for what you need easier).

Now is your time to look at what it is that is taking up precious space in your mind that does not need to be in there. Your mind will clear, and you will feel so much more at peace as you let go one step at a time, of the clutter inside. You are sacred, your mind is sacred. Be conscious of what you allow into that space.

You have your conscious mind and subconscious mind to take care of. Below are some practices you may find helpful in order for you to reduce the clutter in your precious mind. All are listed in my free workbook that you can download at www.divinedeclutteringbook.com.

Below each practice in the workbook is space for you to take notes. You may want to check off each practice you master as you move through your decluttering journey. Once you feel you have mastered one skill or practiced it enough times, move on to another one that calls out to you.

Staying Aware Of And Taking Care Of Your Subconscious Beliefs

No matter how much you want something in life, including a beautifully uncluttered home, you will not receive your desire if your subconscious beliefs are in conflict with what you want. A professional organizer can come into your home, clear it out and make it look perfect. Do not be surprised, however, if after a few months or even a few weeks, the clutter and disorganization is back. The living space that was created by the organizer would not be in alignment with what was inside yourself; so things in your home started to shift back to how they used to be.

One of my first clients was a gentleman who asked me to come into his home to help declutter his bedroom and office area. He was a successful professional yet unhappy in his work, and wanting a relationship and to be married more than anything else. His office space had piles of books and papers covering the circumference of the room along with a lot of unopened mail. We worked incredibly hard over many hours and days to get that space cleared out and all papers into a workable filing system. We also worked together on organizing his bedroom area with the intention that he was going to be having a woman living with him who would need storage space too. We created open spaces to send the message out to the Universe that he was ready to have a woman in his life. He felt really good once these two rooms were arranged in a way to support him. However, when I followed up close to a year later, he told me that he had not kept up with keeping his areas as neat as they were when I left. The clutter started to build again and the open spaces we created in his bedroom were no longer open. He was still unhappy in his work and in dating.

We discussed the idea that there may be some core beliefs about himself, including feeling unworthy, making him unable to move forward and to do exactly what it is that he wanted to do for a career and to be in a long-term relationship. I stressed the importance to him of exploring his unconscious beliefs and to receive support in clearing out the ones that were hurting him and causing him to have repetitive heartbreak in his love life and stress in his work life.

No matter how much he would have offered to pay me to continue to help him clear the clutter in his home, I would have refused at that point, seeing that the clutter was building again. He had to go deeper within himself first, before going into his piles of physical clutter that were getting deeper. I sensed that once he got in touch with those beliefs holding him back, let them go and then filled that space with new and healthy beliefs along with feeling self-love, it would be so much easier to let go of the physical clutter in his home. His new habits of keeping his place neat would also then stick.

I do think it is very good this gentleman got to experience what it was like to have clutter-free rooms created at the time his subconscious beliefs were hurting him, because he could feel how much better he felt in that kind of living space. This gave him the incentive to take the next step to receive the professional help he needed.

I thought about this client in the middle of 2015. This was the time when I chose to take myself though a second decluttering journey after feeling strong energies inside to do this, as I described earlier. My home was quite organized, yet I knew I still had some clutter sitting around and in a few storage boxes...a few things from my past that I knew I needed to let go of and hadn't yet. I thought of how I gave my client from many years back the experience of living in a clutter-free space for a while and that it triggered him to think about some of his core beliefs. I wanted to make sure that my core beliefs were not hurting me in my life.

My inner "Queen" told me that on the first day of my next summer vacation, I was to spend it at a spa in a hotel in the city. This is something I had never experienced before. I had received spa-like treatments before for one hour appointments; however, I never had a spa experience for an entire day and in an upscale setting. I went online to see which hotels in Toronto had spas, and booked to have treatments at one of the top ones located in a luxurious hotel in one of the best parts of the city. Even though the cost of this day would make me go over my spending budget for the month, I did it. "You have to indulge more than you have been. Show your children too, how important it is to treat yourself to exquisite self-care," I told myself.

It was such a huge treat for me and luxurious from the moment I arrived. The concierge took my car and guided me into the spa where I put on the most glorious feeling white robe and slippers they handed to me. The spa was not busy at all that day. In fact, I had the entire change room and hot tub area to myself for the entire morning. The first thing I did when I arrived was shower to wash away the built up stress and exhaustion. I then lay down on the most comfortable foam bed that hugged my body, located in a cozy private space. As I rested, I connected with everything I wanted for myself. It was so wonderful to be able to spend time with myself in such a peaceful feeling place with beautiful soothing music playing and the sounds from the indoor waterfalls.

The next thing I did was step into that hot tub. I allowed the massaging jets to soothe every muscle as each one entered the water. I was alone in that room and I knew the Universe planned it to be that way because as soon as I got in, the tears started to pour out and did not stop. I had never experienced anything like this before. So many feelings coming out at once and some connected to self-worth. I was surprised by it all. It also hit me how hard I had been working and too much, for much of my life; and that I had not been treating myself enough to things and experiences that felt luxurious just as this hot tub felt. I thought I was; however, this experience was telling me that I wasn't, at least not enough.

I had no idea also, that deep down a small part of me was still feeling that I was unworthy of receiving some things that I really wanted for myself. This was such a powerful awakening and so I spent a lot of time in discussion with that part of myself that felt unworthy. I sent so much love to that part of me. I could feel my inner "Queen" so proud that I was finally in touch with that one quiet piece of me that needed so much loving. I could feel my inner "Queen" so proud of me that I was telling that part that she is worthy of everything she wants; and I apologized for ignoring her for much too long. I said to myself, "I'm sorry, I see you and hear you and I love you. Please forgive me, I forgive me, thank you." You can also do this while looking in the mirror any time you feel that a part of yourself needs to be acknowledged, or at times when you feel you haven't treated yourself in a loving way. One of my amazing mentors reminded me of the importance of speaking this way in front of the mirror. It is so powerful.

After a lot of crying, releasing, soothing and unconditional loving of that part of me that was desperate for my attention and love, I got out of the water. I hadn't realized that I spent way too long in there and almost fainted as I stepped out. I was ready to pass out in a way, and wake up to the new me. The one that was so ready to receive my best life! When I felt I could stand up again, I treated myself to something nutritious in the dining area and then went in for my massage and other treatments. They were all so divine!

I ended my day enjoying all of their facilities and lay one last time on that soothing foam bed to just "be." When I was done, I got up and felt ready to get dressed, turn in my robe and slippers and go home. I was ready to open the door of my home in my power with my crown upon my head, step inside feeling my new supportive beliefs with me, more fully connected to all of myself and begin the decluttering; and that is exactly what I did.

The energy that filled me felt like an unstoppable one yet calm and peaceful at the same time. I took action and went through every part of my home one step at a time to make sure that the personal possessions I chose to keep felt to be in alignment with who I felt I was, and what I wanted in my life. I let go of the rest and this felt so freeing! I also shifted from doing even more of what I felt I really wanted to do in my days instead of what I felt I "should" do; and some of that "doing" was actually just "being."

Several months later, I felt completely ready and prepared inside of myself and in my home for something new to enter my life; and I just "let go." It was less than two weeks after that time that I received that most wonderful surprise that I wrote about in the first chapter; and magical things have been happening in my life ever since then...including having my own book, that was my dream, become my reality!

Getting back to my spa experience, as soon as I returned home from the hotel that day, I had the thought to create a package for my clients that would help them get in touch with themselves in the same kind of way I had just experienced. I wanted women to feel what it was like to be removed from their physical clutter for a while as they just became present with themselves. I wanted them to be able to feel parts of themselves that may have been buried in clutter or to discover a part that they may not have known existed. I wanted them to feel as excited and inspired as I did to get the physical clutter out, and really start living in a way that honored their heart and soul and what they want.

After my day away, I found it so much easier to let go of what I knew no longer belonged in my life and wanted this for my beautiful clients. This is when I created my "Divine Destination" decluttering packages which you can learn about at www.divinedeclutteringbook.com. Make it a priority to clear out those subconscious beliefs that are holding you back from having your best life. Honor your authentic self and what it is crying out for. Clear the way and open up space for new beliefs that fully support you in what you wish for. Make self-care your divine responsibility. You deserve and can have whatever it is that you want!

Forgiveness, Releasing Anger, Criticism, Resentment And Guilt

I have one request. If you were to only choose one thing to let go of from your mind right now, let it be all the anger, criticisms, resentments and guilt you are holding on to. By forgiving, you are choosing to break the cycle of pain you have within. Imagine all of the medical problems people suffer. I believe that so many physical ailments arise because of unresolved emotions related to anger, resentment, criticism and guilt from the past. All of these things cause emotional pain; a pain that quietly hums within, like a poison in the body that slowly grows over time if not removed.

During your decluttering journey, your focus will always be about connecting to your self-love and compassion. This is found in your heart space. If you choose to hold on to pain, then you are not taking care of your heart. You are doing yourself great harm. You are the one holding onto the pain, remember this. You are the one suffering, not the one you feel is causing you the pain. Imagine a rope tied tightly around your heart when you have thoughts that cause you to not feel good inside, when thinking of the person you are angry with. This would be severely painful and dangerous for you, wouldn't it? On a physical level, you would be cutting yourself off from your heartbeat and on a spiritual level, from your connection to love.

The way to heal your heart is to set yourself free from that rope; to set yourself free from those "yuk" feelings and thoughts of the other. When you forgive, the rope loosens and you are free. If you feel that you have been holding the person you are angry with as a prisoner with a rope tied around them, you have been incorrect. When you forgive, you set the blocked heart free. The one with the blocked heart is not the other person, it is you. Set yourself free by letting go. You can choose to see everything that you receive in your life as a gift. Be grateful that you have been provided with the gift of forgiveness. When you share your gift, you receive an even greater gift in return...love.

You do not have to come in physical contact if you don't want to, with the person you have in mind that you need to forgive. Thoughts create vibrations and so when you release your thoughts to the Universe, they will reach the person you are thinking of. This is what I want you to imagine: You are alone in a room; the person you are angry with for example, walks into the room you are in, but as a young child. Imagine surrounding both of you in a container of green light of love and compassion. Receive love as you take a breath in. Then as you exhale slowly through your mouth, allow this light to emerge from the ground and rise up to cover you both. Say to this child, "I forgive your true self and release my true self from all pain and suffering. I release myself from all emotional wounds. My heart is now open to give and receive love. The divinity in me greets the divinity in you." If you are wondering whether you have to like this person again, well you don't. You don't even have to think that what they did was now ok, if you feel they caused you harm. You just have to feel peace inside of yourself and remember to let go of what you cannot control.

Emptying Everything Out

What do you carry into the next day? Empty your handbag, pockets and any other carrying cases you use at the end of each day, unless you want to be reminded of and carry energy with you from the day before. File receipts, bills, business cards, etc., and throw out the garbage such as tissues and your children's bandage packaging. Getting the clutter out of your pockets will also help eliminate the clutter from them in your mind. Also, new opportunities will be attacted to, and jump into empty spaces, not filled ones.

Reaching Out

To eliminate cluttering your mind with worry that there is no one around to support you, start to build up a strong support system. I discussed this a little in Chapter 2. Remember also, that until you find support from someone or from a group, you have everything in your home that you have chosen to keep, as support. Remember how your personal possessions can support you in very creative ways. Having this kind of support is no substitute to having unconditionally loving and compassionate people in your life however; so please make a commitment to yourself to also reach out. It is important to express what is inside of you. Expression connects you to your feminine and allows you to release what is in your mind, heart and spirit. Allow yourself to do this in a safe space and with people who you feel safe with.

As you gain support, you may want to offer your own support to others too. Think of something you can do for someone else. Be of service. Even the smallest contribution is acknowledged by the Universe. This can even be sending out kind messages to those you care about. One way that I gave service was to join a support group when I was unhappy in my marriage because when you attend one, you are not just helping yourself, you are helping others. People learn from what you say, and when you help others you will start to feel better yourself too.

Prioritizing

By putting what you need to do in order, from most important to least, you eliminate thought clutter around what needs to be done first. Ask your inner "Queen" each evening what she thinks will be the most important thing you need to do the next day and try to get to that thing first. It is a good idea to complete your highest priority task early in the day because you will probably have the most energy then. When you complete your task early, this will make you feel so good that it will just add to your level of happiness throughout the rest of your day, and probably make you feel even more motivated to get to the next thing you want to get done that day.

Breaking Down Tasks

By breaking down tasks into smaller parts and focusing only on each small part at a time, you will declutter your mind of overwhelming thoughts. Creating files makes piles of paper less overwhelming to deal with; washing the dishes after each meal becomes a pleasure compared to leaving them to do after completing several meals; choosing to declutter only a couple of drawers at a time and keeping the focus there instead of worrying that you need to get the entire room done; and collecting the hair off the bathroom floors after brushing it each morning and night instead of waiting until you decide to clean the bathroom a week or two later will make life easier and feel cleaner for you. I have a difficult time writing when I become focused on how much more I still need to complete. When I keep the focus on what I need to do right now, and keep what I need to do a manageable size, it gets done.

Saying "No"

You will live a miserable life if you try and live it expecting that you can please everyone and do everything that appears in front of you. Focus on what is best for you in your life and learn to say "no" and set boundaries. I suffered as a people pleaser, with little thought about how it would affect my life. I just automatically tried to figure out how I would fit the extra commitments I made into my already filled up days. It was difficult for me to say "no." Well, when I got to my lowest point I finally learned how to say that word. It was really hard to at first, yet it brought huge relief whenever I did.

I also became smarter with my choices in taking on extra responsibilities. My new rule was that if I said "yes" to something, then I had to make sure I took care of my needs first so that I was feeling at my best and not doing for others without fueling myself up first. You cannot give in a healthy way from a vessel running on very low fuel. As the "Queen" of your life you have to practice "healthy selfishness" in order to feel your best and be at your best for others in your life. This means getting comfortable with saying "no" sometimes.

Opening Up Space In Your Schedule

It is much better to have too much time rather than too little time to get things done. Leave space open in your schedule. You will love to know that you have this free space so that you are not always in a rush to get from one activity to the next. A "Queen" in her feminine does not rush. She moves calmly and gracefully in her days. Allow yourself time to rest, meditate, read, become aware of your surroundings when out, notice sequences of events and coincidences, and be present in each moment. Also, it is often during the times when you do nothing that the greatest work is being done for you behind the scenes. I also recommend creating open spaces around your possessions so they have room to breathe, and for the energy to flow.

Embracing Silence

Allow yourself to be silent for at least a few minutes each day. Feel how healing and calming it is. When you are silent, you allow your inner voice to be heard. It is when you are silent that answers come. Whenever you are confused or stressing over an issue and trying hard to figure out the answer or find a solution and can't, try letting all thoughts about it go. Rest for a while and release your thoughts and all the mind chatter as you exhale. Then inhale love. Ask the Universe your questions and trust that you will receive the answers at just the right time. Instead of filling your mind with questions and worry and frustration about an issue, give the Universe the job to figure things out for you. Connect to your inner serenity and peace as you focus on your breath, practice patience and just trust.

Being In Your Feminine And Dreaming During Dull Tasks

Instead of feeling frustrated with tasks that that you find to be boring and time-consuming (such as folding laundry, ironing or washing pots and pans), use these times to feel what you are doing in a sensual way or for dreaming. Get deep into the experience and sink into your feminine, connecting with all of your senses, as your inner masculine does the work...the "doing" part. For example, as you wash the pots, feel every movement your hands make as they scrub each one. Feel the water's gentle touch and listen to the sounds in the sink. Breathe in the scents in the room and take in all that is around you. Feel the beauty and peace of "now." I feel that to be sensual means that you are present with what you are doing, present with life force, taking in life with appreciation in the moment. Sense how you are "being" as you are "doing" things.

The other thing you can do during dull tasks at home that do not require too much focus, is to become present in a dream. Connect to something from your "My Life In Pictures" book. For example, if you are connecting to a picture of you and your love, feel you both together. Imagine your love holding you from behind as you wash the dishes. If you are visualizing your picture of the ocean, imagine feeling the ocean air coming in through the window as you tidy your children's rooms. If you imagine yourself wanting to be taken care of more often, such as receiving regular massages, then move your hands slowly over the washed shirts and pants that need to be flattened out, folded and put away. Connect with how you would feel as someone takes care of your body with their hands as you do this task. This is much more fun and productive to do than filling your mind with things you worry about or feeling frustrated that you have these "chores" to do. The more you connect to your dreams, the more power you give to them; so turn your "chore time" into "treat time!"

Creating Routines

Creating routines and rituals will bring serenity to your days. For example, you can keep your mind clear of what needs to be done by making it routine to write things down regularly such as times for appointments and what you need to buy. You can also practice a regular bedtime routine each night such as putting everything you used and wore for the day in their designated spaces, and having time for other self-care activities such as journaling. You can also think of how you can join one task to the next. For example, while waiting for dinner to cook, you can prepare the shopping list for the next day, make your children's lunches for school or wash up what is in your sink. You can also work on returning things to their designated spots. Think of the routines you create as part of the structure you have built into your home and in your life.

Thinking Less And Just Doing It

Think about how many times you pass the pile of papers sitting in the hallway, or the clothes piled on top of a chair in your bedroom and do nothing about it. Think of how many times you impress on your mind as you look at the objects out of place, that you must put those things away. Think of how you feel each time you see the clutter as you walk by. All of this takes up precious space in your mind. How long do you think it would take to put something away? I suggest that instead of walking by and looking at what needs to be put away, just do it if it will take a short time to! If something belongs on a different floor in your home than the one you are on, think of it as an opportunity to get a little exercise. Practice your sensual walk and take a stroll to the item's designated location. Give the item a heartbeat and feel it thanking you for taking it back to its home.

Now that you have been provided with some suggestions on how you can take care of your precious mind, I hope that you begin practicing some of them. If your mind showed up as one of the rooms in your home, what would it look like? I imagine my space feeling bright with white walls, soft plush white rugs over a white wash wooden floor, and a glass ceiling so that I could see the beautiful sky and stars at night. I also picture interesting light fixtures with white feathers and crystal.

If you had clutter in that room (thought clutter), what would it look like? I see all of my thought clutter as floating dark bubbles. I would want all the floating clutter bubbles out so that they do not distract my view of the sky. I would want to be able to enjoy the night sky and connect to the thought that my life is filled with as many possibilities as there are stars. I see that there is a window in my room. I have the ability to open it to let the bubbles move out so that my space becomes clear. I'd want them to float up into the sky, pop and disappear as they get close to the sun. I would want my clutter to go.

Using imagery may help you as you make the choice to either remove something from your mind that you know is not serving you well, or not...and just as I've finished typing the word "not," the word "naughty" came to mind. It is fun to be "naughty" sometimes, isn't it, in certain situations, if you know what I mean? Thinking of your clutter issue though, I know you've been doing some "naughty" things in your days. Putting one sexy leg in front of the other, please take your steps into the next chapter if you are ready to see what some of these things are...

CHAPTER 8
You Will Remove
Your Little Naughty Habits

Now that you have taken your brave steps into this chapter, I want you to relax and trust that all you have done in your life up until this point in time has been ok...even though I have written in my title that you have been "naughty." Remember to practice unconditional loving of yourself. I used the word "naughty" in this title because I want you to keep connected to your feminine and having fun as you declutter your life! I've chosen this title to catch your attention and keep things light! Your feminine goddess self is made up of a range of energies including one that may be more mysterious, playful, very sexy, dominant perhaps and possibly a little naughty yet in a very fun and healthy way ... whatever that looks like for you.

Remember to enjoy and express all aspects of your feminine because all parts are beautiful ... and in a relationship, a person who enjoys being in their masculine will very much appreciate feeling all of your different energies of the glorious radiant divine feminine. Give your love this gift, even before this divine soul arrives, if you are still not yet together in physical reality.

Now before reading any further, I want you to close your eyes for a moment, and connect with your inner "Queen" and listen to her express to you whatever it is you feel she needs to at this time. Feel how she soothes you and makes you feel that everything is and will work out just the way you wish things to, or even better, as you continue to let go of your clutter inside and out. Perhaps she will even ask you if you feel there is something you want to express through your feminine that you have not yet. Then take some time and express to her. You can even use your mirror to do this exercise and make it one of your healthy habits.

Write down whatever comes up for you, including some things you may want to try, to continue to expand being in your feminine. Maybe it is something "naughty" and fun you want to do in a visualization. Remember that what you visualize and feel will begin the creation of it, so make it decadent and delicious! Use your free workbook that you can download at www.divinedeclutteringbook.com to write the description of your fun visualization that came up as you connected to your feminine.

Now to get back to your "naughtiness" with your clutter...some of the clutter in your life may not just have to do with what you have around you in your personal space and in your mind. You could be suffering from habits that take up a lot of your time and cause you frustration. Habit clutter is one form of non-physical clutter. Wouldn't you rather have time to do what you truly want to do for yourself... like perhaps take more time to rest and "just be" and practice connecting to your feminine in all the ways you wish to?

You will have more time to do what you want once you let go of some of your non-physical clutter habits. I suggest that you read through all of the habits below and select one you want to work on eliminating first. Then when you feel ready, select another naughty habit to eliminate. If not sure which one to choose, ask your inner "Queen" for guidance. Not all habits listed below may be relevant for you. If you feel there is something you do that I did not list, then write it down and think of what you can do in its place that feels healthier to you. You will also notice that I touched on some of the items discussed, earlier on in my book. Repetition of new material is a good thing for the memory.

All naughty habits are listed in my free workbook that you can download at www.divinedeclutteringbook.com with space also provided for you to take your own notes. The best part of choosing to eliminate some of the habits that are not serving you well in your daily routine is that you will not miss them! Your time and your mind are both precious and sacred. Make sure that what you do with your time and what you fill your mind with, respects your own preciousness and sacredness.

Taking In Negativity At Sunrise

Instead of watching TV and listening to the news in the morning, enjoy some quiet time while you eat. Connect with how you feel you want your day to look like. If you have your family at the table, focus on them instead of on the TV. You can also relax and be present with your pet next to you. While in the car, pay attention to how your mood changes based on the music you choose to listen to. It is best to start your day in the best feeling state possible so think twice before you decide to turn on other voices such as the news while driving first thing in the morning. Remember that you are trying to remove negativity from your mind; so if you feel you watch a lot of programs or listen to news reports first thing that get you down, or listen to music with messages that don't feel good to you, this is just adding to what you want to remove.

It is important to keep up with what is going on in the world; however, you have the choice as to when in the day you tune in and for how long you do. It is also ok to take out lots of time for yourself and get your own life in order, and tune out the rest of the world for a while. Sometimes this is needed. Also trust that what you need to know, you will find out about somehow. The message will be brought to you. Sometimes it is hard to really connect with what you need for yourself and how you are feeling when bombarded with outside noise, so go ahead and turn it all off for now.

Disturbing Your Peace

Do you read the newspaper in the morning with your breakfast? Does it make you feel good as you read through? If it doesn't, then put it down. It is important to keep up with the news; however, if you already have too much that does not feel good inside of you that you are trying to let go of, then stay away from more that does not make you feel well, as I discussed above. Instead of reading the paper, choose to express some positive affirmations like ones you say to yourself in the mirror, or read a little from a book you love. You can also send out loving energy from your heart space to people and places you have concern for in the world to add to the good feeling energy in this Universe, instead of sitting in energy that brings you down.

I learned that the better I am feeling throughout each day, the better it is for others, as the good feeling energy I radiate affects others. You may find that on days you are feeling your best that people come up to you or smile at you as you walk by. This is because they feel your happy vibes. Don't allow the negativity you read cause you to focus on it all day and destroy the opportunity of you gifting others with your radiant energy. Be responsible for the energy you radiate out. Shine your light!

Filling Your Schedule Incorrectly

If you have committed to something out of the goodness of your heart but feel that you really do not have time to do this, then express this and decide what to do. It is very important to remember that you have to take care of yourself first. Once you have your life and schedule under control, you will have plenty more time to commit to doing things for others, but right now you need to focus on what you need to do for you. You have to have trust that when you give something up, like a commitment you prefer not to have right now, you are making space for someone else to enter and do what you could not do. Do not commit to something if what you choose to do leaves you with feelings of resentment, anger, pressure and exhaustion. Do not say "yes" to others if you feel it results in you saying "no" to you.

Here are some examples of things you may need to eliminate:

- driving carpool as often as you are
- being active on certain social media sites
- taking on extra projects at work when you are already overloaded
- going out with someone who brings you down
- the amount of time you spend talking on the phone or text messaging
- the number of times in your day you check your voice mail, social media sites and email messages (and I suggest you turn off the notification sounds so that you don't feel the urge to look at each message that comes in at every moment)

Make a list of things you feel you want to eliminate doing and then take action. Eliminate one thing at a time. I still remember the first time I said "no" to a co-worker when I was asked to take on an extra project at work. It felt so empowering to do this!

As far as checking your devices for texts and emails, I recommend taking care of your needs first which means getting ready for your day in the morning, eating a healthy meal and doing your most important task that you know you want to get done first thing. Then once you have completed what you need to do for your own self-care, go ahead and check your devices.

I also suggest choosing a specific number of times in the day that you check email, search the web or use social media sites for example, because they can be huge time wasters and ways for you to procrastinate on what you know you want to get done. Also have a time limit for these things.

Going To Bed Late

Sleep is so important. Focus on getting more sleep by going into bed a little earlier. If you are going to bed late then you are probably waking up late, or having to wake up early and feeling exhausted. Wouldn't you prefer waking up feeling refreshed and with an early start so that you feel you have a full day to do what you want to do and don't feel rushed?

For those of you with young children, I know how difficult it is to get to bed early when there are probably many things for you to still tend to once the kids are in bed. I can almost guarantee you that when you start to eliminate some of your naughty habits, you will see that time opens up in your life and you may be able to get in bed earlier and also have more energy to get up earlier.

I also believe that if you truly want to do something, you will make it happen with zero excuses. A "Queen" in her power does not make excuses. I try to wake up earlier than my girls most mornings and stay in bed to do something healthy for myself first, such as write a little. I then take a few moments for meditation to get centered and to focus in on my plan for the day. Since starting to meditate (and there are many different kinds of meditations, where you may choose to be silent or even speak softly about whatever you wish, so do what feels good to you) and listening to my inner voice, I've found that I make it through busy days feeling much more relaxed and energetic. You may want to try this too.

I am also quite strict with myself when it comes to my bedtime routine and try to get to bed at a decent hour at least a few times a week. My daughters know when "Queen Mommy Time" starts. It begins after our dance party. We put on our favorite music and dance up a storm for about twenty minutes before bedtime and have tons of fun! Dancing is a fabulous way to connect to your feminine and get your creative energy flowing (which I have discussed already in an earlier chapter), and also an amazing way to shift your vibration. When you shift your vibration you attract different things to you...and better things as you feel better with what you are doing that moment. Also, when you dance you can easily let go of the worry from your day as you connect to the music and the sensual flow of your body. When you let go of worry, and all else that does not feel good, your vibration goes back to its natural best feeling state. When you let go, you become open to receiving.

Let me give you an example... sometimes I'd get frustrated when a call I am waiting for does not come in at the time I was expecting it to, or a package in the mail does not arrive on time. I have spent countless hours worrying about things like this that I cannot control. What I have found is that when I let go of the worrying and stop thinking about what I want, the call suddenly comes in and the package is waiting for me in the mailbox the next day. My worry was keeping what I wanted from coming to me. I put energy into those thoughts and the Universe responded by giving me more to worry about. Now I know in times of worry, to shift to trusting that I will receive everything in the best of timing, and to put my focus back on what I am doing that present moment. I "let go." Magic happens when you do this so I hope you give it a try! Think of the word "release," because it has the word "ease" in it. Believe that after you "release," things you want will come to you with "real ease."

When our dance party is done, my girls get ready for bed and once I settle them in on a typical night when I am home, "my time" begins. They know that during this time their mama is getting their home in order and she is doing good things for herself, practicing "healthy selfishness." They know that I'm throwing in laundry, putting the clean dishes from the dishwasher away so that it is empty for the morning, and then in my quiet space to be present to do those things that are important to do for me before I go to sleep. I do whatever feels best to do each evening and do not pressure myself to do anything, because some evenings I just want to get in bed and sleep! Be easy on yourself and do what feels best for you, always. Do more of what you "want to" do instead of feeling like you "have to" do anything. I just have to say though, that having a regular routine is important and powerful for success; so if you really want something, try keeping your regular routine as best you can.

You, as the "Queen" of your life, need a good sleep and deserve to end your day doing something that connects you to your heart and soul such as journaling, writing what you are thankful for and just "being," for some examples. Choose to do something that feels really freeing, peaceful and honoring to your authentic self. Also, when you feel tired, imagine that your body and the Divine are expressing something to you. They could be telling you to stop and to rest because perhaps the Universe needs you to get out of its way so that it can do something for you. Stop when tired instead of pushing yourself. Choose to see that you live in a fully supportive and loving Universe. You don't have to feel like you have to do it all, so rest and trust that the Divine will do its part to take care of some things for you and will help make things happen in the best way for you. Just like having that package arrive, that phone call come in and answers appear to the questions you had been struggling to find yet could not. Ask the Universe for what you want. Let go of your control, relax your body, become soft on the outside, open your palms, surrender and sleep.

Your Negative Talking

Speaking badly about others does not look good for you and is not good for you. Instead, choose to express kindly and if you have nothing kind to say, choose to say nothing. The kind words you use will send out good vibes and will attract something that feels good to you. Tell people you interact with, such as cashiers at stores, to have a great day. This should help you have a great day too. When someone asks how you are feeling, get used to saying you feel terrific instead of "not bad." What you say will impact how you feel.

If you choose words to express that make you feel really good, and use them often, you will start to feel the difference inside of you. I am in no way telling you to avoid how you feel when feeling anything but happy. That is pushing back down into your clutter what you must pull out to see, honor, be fully present with and then release. It is so important to express your emotions as a human being and also as a feminine woman. Choose who you do this with wisely. Express what you feel to those you are close with and trust, to your higher power and in your writing. It is only by facing what it is that is bothering you, that you can start to feel better and heal.

Expressing Critical And Sarcastic Remarks

Criticizing and expressing in a sarcastic way are unhealthy habits. Instead of using sarcasm or being critical, think of something kind to say or say nothing. When you feel a criticism coming on, look at what it is and see if this is something inside of you that perhaps you need to deal with. Sarcasm can be a sign of anger you hold inside of your own self about something. It reflects poorly on you when you put others down, even if it is in a funny kind of way through sarcasm. Therefore, avoid these kinds of remarks as they are not only hurtful to you and the one you project your remark on, but also send out a vibration into the Universe that will attract to you something on the same wavelength. The energy that you release outwards comes back to you, so make sure that what you give out you want back. Use this time instead to send out kind and loving thoughts and words to others.

Focusing On What You Don't Want

I've written earlier on how important it is to express what you do want, especially once you know what it is that you don't want, so choose to do this. Make this your healthy habit. As you learn to spend less time in thoughts of what it is that you do not want in your life and get in the habit of focusing and speaking about what you do want, you will see how life will bring to you what you want.

Be a dreamer, be true to yourself and express exactly what you want for yourself and your home, no matter how different it may be from what your life looks like right now. By reducing the amount of time you focus on and speak about what you don't like or want, you free up space inside of you and in your day to speak of something better.

When in long line ups, on hold on the phone, or in traffic for example, use these times to express quietly or out loud all that you desire. Get used to connecting with all of your desires and speaking about them easily, feeling that you can have them and that they are coming to you. For example, you may want to say, "I am in the active process of creating my clutter-less life and all I want is already on its way to me. I am so excited to receive _____ and I am completely ready for _____ to happen. I am already getting my (name the room in your home) cleared out and I am feeling better and better each day with every small step I take. I love myself and I am giving myself what my heart and soul are asking for. I am unapologetically creating my home and life to be just as I imagine it to be."

Showing Up Late

Instead of arriving late to places you are expected to be at, arrive early. By doing this, you will have some time to relax, breathe or perhaps do some reading. You may find that you are never on time, arriving late and in a panic. Why do you do this? Take some time and think about this. Perhaps you do not like being early because the feelings of waiting trigger something that doesn't feel good from you past, held inside of you. Maybe you were always kept waiting by your mother when you were young, and being late is one way to express your anger from your past or avoid those feelings that would come up with waiting. Once you understand your reason for your behavior, it will be easier to move to a healthier choice. Perhaps you know that arriving early or on time is healthy for you, but you feel you do not deserve to feel this way so you make yourself late. Next time you have somewhere to go, leave thirty minutes earlier and see what happens. Connect with your inner "Queen" as soon as you arrive and see if she has something to tell you.

When I go to appointments I like to arrive early. Life feels very rushed sometimes and so I feel it is a treat to arrive early to appointments to just relax and breathe. One of my favorite things to do in the day, and as I wait for appointments or for my children to come out of their after school programs, is to stay present and see what "signs" the Universe shows me. This makes me trust that things in life are happening "for me" in the best way, instead of "to me" in a hurtful way. When I become quiet and present during these waiting times, and just look out, I often notice or hear something that catches my attention. These things that I see or hear are what I call "signs" to remind me that nature and the Universe are my partners and taking action to help me create what I want. As I take one step forward doing something good for myself and for my home, so does the Universe.

I may see something that is symbolic of the Divine or known to be good luck, or something that triggers some of my dreams. It may be a white feather, penny, heart, ladybug, butterfly, painting on the wall that reminds me of something in "My Life In Pictures" book, or a little girl wearing a tiara. I may also notice words of background music playing or of someone else speaking in the room and hear them as loving messages for me. I tend to receive many messages through personalized car licence plates as I drive which are really fun to spot as my eyes move to them!

I love noticing the signs and synchronicities each day that show me that life loves me. I also enjoy writing them down sometimes. I could write pages and pages right now of the incredible signs I have received over the years that have inspired me to keep on my healthy path and see life through eyes of love instead of fear. The more energy you give to what feels good, the more you feed that energy and the more you will receive in that energy.

I suggest that you purchase a small notepad this week and keep it with you wherever you go, and write down messages you receive from the Universe and in nature as you go about your day. Writing is powerful. Make this a fun activity for yourself and if you want, share this idea with a close friend and then share the gifts you each received in your days! Remember to say "thank you" whenever you notice something you see as a "sign," along with "I am open to receiving more wonderful signs, I love you."

Believing There Are No Solutions

Instead of fearing that there are no solutions to your problems or a way of getting out of the massive pile of "stuff" you have, trust that there is always a solution and a healthy way out. Nothing is impossible. Think of the famous quote by Audrey Hepburn, "Nothing is impossible, the word itself says 'I'm possible'." Thoughts that bring you down also bring your energy level down. Notice how your energy and mood change when you choose thoughts that make you feel good.

I remember someone telling me this a long time ago, "God will never give you more than you can handle." If you trust in this statement, then you can relax. Worrying is wasting precious energy that could be used for something productive. There will always be a solution available, just like there will always be time for what you need to get done because time expands. When you are confused and trying to figure something out with many choices spinning in your mind, allow these times to signal you to let your thoughts go and to rest. Hand over your overwhelming worries and confusions to your Creator and allow the Divine to take care of things, as I discussed earlier. Answers come in silence, not with the noise you create in your mind.

Your Unproductive Conversations

Have you ever thought of what you speak about most often? Do you talk a lot about things such as the weather, the government's actions, other people's problems, gossip you heard about one of your friends or the price of gas? All of these topics are things that you cannot control. Think of the emotions that you create and how your body reacts as you talk about things like this or other subjects that are out of your control. Does it feel good to you? If not, then don't talk about these things.

In addition, if you don't have as much time in your days as you would like to have to get things done, then shorten the times you express to others by making sure that what you express feels good and is not filled with discussion of things you cannot control. Since you can't do anything about those subjects, why would you want to spend your precious time discussing them for as long as you do? It would be a more productive use of your time to practice speaking about things you can control, what you are actively doing in your life, those you love and things you love. Also, when you eliminate some of your talking you have more time to allow the person you are speaking with to express whatever they choose to. Practice being a compassionate and present listener and the best support for those you love and enjoy spending time with. It is also important to think about who you spend your time with and remove yourself from toxic relationships and those who you feel are not healthy for you and your life.

Your mood may have just shifted from reading the sentence above if you do have a toxic person or people in your life. You may need support to help you if you do. To cheer you up for the moment though, I have good news...the final three chapters are going to be very exciting for you! They will be describing what you need to do to get all of your physical clutter out from each room, and provide you with instructions on how to transform your home to become your beautiful, safe feeling and sacred space...a space that is in harmony with the sacred divine feminine being you are!

Leaving all "naughty" thoughts and habits behind and with your sparkling crown upon your head, please go ahead and practice your powerful and confident "Queen's" stride into the next chapter...

CHAPTER 9
You Will Follow These Oh So Lovely Orders

I hope you enjoyed your walk into this new chapter! You have arrived to the entryway of the start of a new chapter of your life because this is the place where you are going to start to move your physical clutter out... the time has come! You have covered a lot of material on non-physical clutter to this point and now I am sensing you are starting to feel a little better inside as you have started to clear out some of your inner "stuff." As you continue to remove your inner clutter, take better care of what you choose to keep in your mind and do in your days for healthy habits, and with the loving support of your divine inner "Queen," I believe you will have a much easier time to now deal with letting go of your physical clutter. What do you think? By the way, there is no best way on how to clear your clutter; all I can do is give you some suggestions as you are a unique soul and only you know what is best for you. You can start with the non-physical then get to the physical, or do it in reverse, or do a bit of both at a time which is what I suggest you try. This is why I recommended in the first chapter, that you read through this entire book first and then go back and select what you feel you would like to work on and in what order. All you have to do is continue checking in with your inner "Queen," as she will guide you.

The time has finally come to confront all of your personal possessions surrounding you in your home... the ones you wish to keep and the ones that your inner "Queen" knows need to go. However, before you begin this royal mission, you are going to prepare for yourself a very special space that will be just for you and only you. It is important to give yourself gifts and I hope you find this one to be one of your favorites that you cherish. If you are ready for this gift, connect with the true you that you found in the mirror and please read on...

You Will Create Your Sacred Space

To me, the meaning of a sacred space is a location where you can retreat to in order to connect to your divine self... a place where you can find the true you over and over again. This is the part of you that may have been aching expression for a very long time yet has been suffocating in a pile of your clutter so you could never reach her. The clutter could be worry of what other people may think of you if you fully expressed your authentic self, or it could be anger or fear built up from your past which is making you hesitant to express your true nature and receive your desires. It could even be your very strong inner critic not allowing you to have the life you want, or it could be something else. This is the place where you will find her (in addition to seeing her in the mirror) and where she will feel safe. This is also the place where you will love connecting with source energy as you connect through your heart and relax. You can try meditating here and sitting in silence to receive wisdom and answers to the questions you have, especially questions you have as far as which area to declutter next. Or you may choose to do a meditation using your voice. With your eyes closed, softly express outloud what you need from the Divine or from your Inner Queen. Surrender and say for example, "I love you, please help me, I don't know what to do right now. Thank you." Expose your palms to be in the position to receive. If it feels relaxing for you, continue repeating your statement because it will help shift your focus away from other thoughts that don't make you feel good.

I want you to give yourself the gift of having one of these spaces set up in your home if you do not already have this. Ultimately, my wish for you, as you remove the clutter step by step from each of your rooms, is that you claim each new decluttered space to be sacred. I want you to feel like you can connect with your heart and spirit easily, wherever you are in your home; and eventually also when you go out.

Having a sacred space created in your home is a wonderful "escape" to retreat to, especially when you want to remove yourself from the noise and hustle and bustle going on in other parts of your home made by everyone else there. It will also make you feel really good to have this space to enjoy while the rest of your home is still filled with the clutter, especially at those times when you feel very stressed and out of control due to it all.

Your job now is to look around your home and decide where you want your sacred space to be. You only need a very small area because all you will need there is something to rest some of your favorite things on (that I will discuss next), and a large comfortable cushion to sit on, or a chair or your couch. Once you have located your space I want you to think about clearing the energy from there as you want it to feel as fresh and empty as possible so that the area is fully ready and available to receive all of you. Be creative with how you feel you can clear the energy from that space. You can use ideas from Feng Shui if you like.

What I like to do is open the windows in the room then clap my hands in front of me as I walk around the entire space, remembering to clap also into every corner and visualize all the stagnant and old energies leaving out the window. Even if you have chosen a room that still has not been cleared of the clutter to create your sacred space in, that is ok. Move the old non-physical energy out even with the physical old energy clutter still there. Believe that the movement you are creating by the clapping will help in the process of physically removing the clutter from that room when you are ready to do that. Imagine that the new energy you are now going to be creating in that room, with your sacred space, will be out of alignment with the energy of the items your inner "Queen" knows need to be removed. This will make it much easier for you to clear the old items out, as you begin to sense the contrast in energies.

As the old heavy energy moves out with your clapping, feel the space being filled with love and light that comes from the Universe and from inside of your heart. Next, I suggest you fill a small dish with sea salt and place it in the location where your sacred space will be. Think of this salt as a deep cleanser for this space. I like to leave the salt there overnight and then discard it. Do what feels best for you.

The final step I enjoy (and I suggest you only do what feels best and enough for you, and perhaps just the clapping will be enough) is to burn sage and set intentions as I walk around with it, allowing the smoke to enter all areas I want to clear old energy out from (including in drawers and cupboards). I do not recommend doing this however, if you have children or others in your home that are sensitive or allergic to sage or smoke. As you burn the sage and walk through your space, connect with your creator and your inner "Queen." Set the intention that all remaining old and stagnant energies that have not been serving you well are removed.

Ask to let go of everything that is not in alignment with the truth of who you are and with your highest good. You can say statements such as "I am releasing all fears that I feel I have inside of me," "I am removing all yukky thoughts and judgement about myself," and "I am letting go of all anger connected to my past." You can then ask that your space be filled with everything you want and that serves your higher purpose such as unconditional love, peace, light, health, creativity, abundance, joy, intimacy, harmony and fun. Write down some of your statements and what you are asking for in my free workbook that you can download at www.divinedeclutteringbook.com. When finished, put out the sage stick, trusting that all has been done for you. Express thanks for the loving support you are receiving and for your sacred home.

Now, if you are someone who likes a little extra special something sometimes, like whipped cream and a cherry on top of your ice cream, you may enjoy just one final step as a treat. You can top off your energetically fresh and clean space with a spritz of lavender oil. This oil will add to the freshness of the space and can be thought of as an invitation for good Chi to enter.

You are now ready to design and decorate your sacred space! I have always had mine in the bedroom and used the surface of a wooden piece of furniture. I would either sit on the couch next to it or on the bed (depending on which home I was in as I have moved about every two years since I left my marriage), and each room was set up differently. If you do not have a small table or other piece of furniture to use, find an empty box, crate or bin, place a pretty scarf over it, and voila! You may then want to sit on a large cushion to be at a comfortable height to your table surface instead of higher up on a chair.

The next step is the best part because you get to choose what you would like to display on your surface. Remember that this space is one that will allow you to easily connect with your heart and spirit and so you want to choose items that will help you in this way. Ask your inner "Queen" what she feels she would like in that space. For example, she may remind you of something you have from your childhood that you love and have kept all of these years in a box. You may want to ask yourself why you have kept that item for so long. You may want to place that object on your table and perhaps it will become the inspiration for something you want to create in your life. It may be connected to your purpose.

A candle is always a good idea to display and light as part of your ritual to welcome yourself to your time there. You may want to display a photo of someone you admire, a place you want to travel to or anything else that brings out the best thoughts and feelings in you. I also like to have a very soft throw blanket in the space to wrap around myself and connect this to the love I feel from the Universe gift wrapped around me. Having a bouquet of fresh flowers is also a decadent treat.

My inner "Queen" told me when I woke up one morning in the basement apartment many years ago, to purchase certain spices and mix them together in a little container and place them in my sacred space and so I did. I remember some of the spices being turmeric, saffron (both of which I had never used before and didn't even know what they looked like) and cinnamon. When I mixed them together and took in the delicious aroma, all of a sudden I had interesting memories come up from certain times in my life which were very helpful to connect with. I was then curious to know the symbolic meanings of some of the spices as I felt this may enlighten me further on something I needed to know about myself.

Having an object for each of the senses in your sacred space would be something your feminine would love. Choose items to look at, smell, touch, listen to and perhaps even taste. I enjoy listening to the sounds of the ocean and birds on recordings. My spirit loves to be by the ocean, and I immediately slide into a very relaxed state when I hear the sound of the water.

Try meditation or something else that makes your soul feel happy (as every soul is unique and needs something different). Change what you have on your table when you feel the urge to and most importantly, just "be" in this space. Even if you feel like having nothing but a candle there, that is great too! You may not want to have the distraction of objects around you. Feel yourself connected with the earth as you connect with your heart and soul. Feel how peaceful and joyful you can become just by breathing and "being."

Close your eyes, breathe in love from the Divine through the top of your head and feel it radiate through every part of your body. Then as you exhale, feel love radiate outward through your heart as you open it up, imagining you are unwrapping your sacred gift to share. As you do this you may come to realize that you do not need "things" to make you feel loved, blissful or joyful. Think of this as you declutter; also remembering that what you radiate outwards comes back to you.

When you have completed designing your royal retreat that I hope you enjoy visiting often, you will be ready to move on and begin the glorious task of removing the physical clutter and getting organized in the rest of your home! You have learned in the previous chapters how to bring yourself into the best feeling place to gracefully and easily do this, by connecting with your feminine and dreams. You now also have all the information you need for creating fresh spaces in all of your rooms and locations, such as in a drawer.

Once you get the clutter out from a location remember to clap, state what you want, place salt in the area, sage and spritz. The space will then be happy and ready to receive whatever you choose to put in there. Make sure that what you put in that space feels like it aligns with the love you filled that area with...which is the love inside of you. Remember to keep things that align with your best self. Are you ready to begin your physical decluttering? If your inner "Queen" is giving her most vibrantly glorious sign of a "YES" to you, then with your most beautiful smile on your face, please read on...

You Will Have Only Divinely Designated Places For Papers

I want you to imagine the most organized efficient office manager wearing a striking outfit and gorgeous heels that bring out her feminine flare, in charge of all the details and papers for one of the top organizations on this planet. Now imagine that this woman is you. What do you think you would have to do differently from what you are doing today in order to succeed in that job? I am giving you the opportunity right now to get excited about clearing all surfaces and drawers of loose papers and finding appropriate places for them so that you begin to feel like this office manager, but one that works from home.

For this book, I will be suggesting the most simplified, low tech and inexpensive ways to start to get your papers in order. If you are someone who is really struggling with a huge pile of paper clutter and need to get them in order quickly, and also are not very comfortable with learning how to scan and store documents on computer, then you will have something to try that hopefully will make you feel at ease instead of stressed due to having to get into "technical" talk. This will be your first step in the process to be able to experience how you feel with this level of organization.

I find when working with clients that each one likes to do something different with their papers; however, most everyone has benefitted from what I describe below. Your new homes for most of your papers will be located in the following divine nine districts:

1. Box For Files
2. Binder For Papers
3. Bin For Tax Purposes
4. Binder For Recipes
5. Back Of Cupboard
6. Baggie For Coupons
7. Bin For Children
8. Bookshelf For Reading Material
9. Bag For Recycling

1. Box For Files

I find that the best way to store important papers so that they are available when needed, yet not referred to very often, is in filing drawers. I recommend using individual locking plastic filing drawers as they are light to carry, can be stacked and easily moved around. In my home I have one drawer and that is enough for my personal files.

As far as how you set up your files in the box, everyone will have their own opinion as to what they feel will work best for them, so do what you feel will work best for you. I believe the important thing to focus on at this time is just to get your papers into their proper homes. Later on you can decide if you want to hang your files or not, if your filing box has the option for both. You can also decide if you want to have files grouped together based on categories or filed alphabetically.

I have had several clients call me to tell me that they need support either in person or while on Skype with me to get their papers into the proper files. I learned that these clients had unpleasant feelings connected to some bills and documents arriving in the mail, and even to the name on the file that the document had to go into. This caused them to delay opening mail and/or living with stacks of papers sitting around their home that made their stomach turn.

Imagine how you would feel if every day you walked by a pile of papers on your entryway table on a subject that you imagine not liking to think about, such as for example a debt, legal papers from a divorce or parking fines. How do you think this would take away or add to your day? It is really important to remove those papers that make you feel uneasy or upset in any way, especially when not planning on dealing with them that moment or if they are ready to be filed yet haven't been, so that you can stay in a good feeling place. To start to think about a bill at the moment you walk by it, may trigger frustration about money; this would be thought clutter. There is no need for you to think about this bill if you are not taking action with it that moment so it is best to store it in a place out of view yet in a location that you can easily get to, which will be discussed further down.

In order to solve my clients' frustrations and fears with opening their mail and filing papers, we created new names to label the file folders. This gave them some relief. Just by choosing a different file name, they felt more comfortable as they filed their papers and also had an easier time opening mail. They also tried as best they could to think of something pleasant and were thankful for with each piece of paper they picked up to file, in order to continue the shift in their energy to a better feeling place.

While labeling your files, come up with names that make you feel your best and at the same time clearly define the papers stored inside. Below are a few examples of subjects you may want to create files for. In brackets are examples of alternative names for labeling the files in case the subject name makes your tummy feel weak and you are looking for a name that brings on better feelings. Be creative and come up with names that you like! It is important that the sexy sorting secretary/office manager of the home is feeling fabulous as she sorts through mail and looks through her files, so do all you can to stay in that energy and label things wisely. I suggest going through your files once a year and clearing out what you no longer need. You will find space to create your own names for your files in my free workbook that you can download at www.divinedeclutteringbook.com.

- car ownership information *(My Hot Rod Ownership)*
- car insurance *(My Hot Rod Protection)*
- medical info for you/family members *(Well-Being For (name of each person on each file))*
- credit cards *(Loaned Money Gift From (name the credit card))*
- parking/speeding tickets paid *(Rules Of The Road I Follow)*
- life insurance *(My Radiant Life Plan)*
- health insurance *(My Radiant Health Plan)*
- home insurance *(My Healthy Home Plan)*
- home mortgage/rent *(My Sacred Home Plan)*
- report cards for kids *(Mini Me's Performance Info)*
- passports *(Sacred Escape Tool)*
- birth certificates *(Entrance Proof Into This Divine World)*
- home appliances warrantees *(My Divine Home's Necessity Plans)*
- *about my pet (My Four Paws' File)*
- everything else (*Divinely Disordered*)

  This is a file for odds and ends on various topics that you will probably not need to refer to again yet feel are important to keep at this time.

As you start going through your papers and creating files, make it a sacred event. Prepare yourself for this sacred task by following some of my suggestions on how to get into your feminine first. Shower and wash yourself slowly, imagining that the water pouring down on you is the love from the Universe showering you, moisturize your body in a sensual way and massage each finger knowing that they will be creating sacred organized spaces. Then get dressed up into something that adds to the beauty you feel inside yourself, knowing you will be doing something so good for you. Put on your crown. Turn on the music. Dance a little first. Imagine your inner "Queen" fully present and supporting you. Connect with all the gifts of your feminine and transmute this energy into sorting power!

Now if you want this sacred event to get a little sexy and hot, then imagine the love of your life in the picture if you are in a relationship or interested in being in one. Go ahead and have some fun! Visualize your love in the room, supporting you in any way you fantasize about, as you begin your task. Your partner may be holding you from behind as you go through your pile of clutter on the counter, or may have their fingers running through your hair as you are filing your papers, or may whisper something into your ear about the reward you will receive when you are all done. Connect with how you feel as you imagine each scenario.

Remember that how you feel will attract things to you that resonate with that feeling vibration so connect with exactly what it is you would like, and that makes you feel fabulous! Make sure though, that the action you are taking to let go of your clutter and sort is something you are doing for you, and always for you, no matter how good of a reward you imagine receiving. Do not do something just to please your partner. You must make yourself happy first and make good and healthy choices for you. Keep the focus on you, and do what is best for you. What is good for you will affect others in your life in a wonderful way. The best part is that if you are in a relationship yet unhappy with the quality of intimacy you have together, instead of focusing on what is not good and complaining about that, visualize what it is that you do want, and do this as you take action. This will help shift your reality. Give it a try and see what you bring to your life!

As you move forward with the physical decluttering of everything else in your home, I hope that you enjoy my suggestions so that you have sacred, sensual, sexy and super powerful fun in the process! It is really important to play a lot in life. Make this part of your play time! Please keep all of my suggestions in the front of your mind as you continue to read and let go of your "stuff," right up until the last page of this book and right up until the moment you get rid of your last piece of clutter! Ask your inner "Queen" to remind you of what you need to do at times you feel you are struggling in the process. Always remember to ask for help when needed as you take action, and keep this book handy to refer to regularly along with my free workbook (that you will have filled in) that you can download at www.divinedeclutteringbook.com.

2. Binder For Papers

This is my most favorite paper storing system. I have been using it for many years and I call it my "Peace of Mind Binder" because it truly brings me feelings of peace as I use it and look at it. It is probably the simplest and least expensive kind of organizing system I can suggest and a good place to start as you practice keeping your papers in order. This is simply splendid for the busy "Queen." You are going to create a beautiful binder of a home for those papers you need to save for tax purposes, for all other papers that come in monthly that you like to keep track of such as electricity bills (and it is great if you receive your bills online as this will save you storage space) and other odds and ends that you need to refer to such as your children's after school program information pages and some other things I will describe further down. This is what you will need to get started:

- One large three-ring binder that zips closed
- Letter size binder plastic page protectors (you can find them in packages of at least 10 at a dollar store) or for the more expensive option use letter size slide-lock binder pouches with easy to use zipper closure
- One package of binder pockets
- Sticky tabs that you will label and then attach to the plastic pages

- Business card holder pages
- Several pieces of three hole paper

I like to use a binder that I can zip closed. I find it relaxing to look at because all papers are hidden when it is zipped up and it can be transported easily without the chance of things falling out. I am not suggesting a fancy system for paper storage or to keep track of things on electronic devices at this time because, as I had mentioned earlier, I am writing this for the woman who wants to start with the basics, something that is inexpensive and who also may not feel comfortable using electronic devices. So do not feel that you have to be up to date with the "latest" in technology in order to feel that you are truly organized. You can function at your best using the simplest of systems.

You will probably find that over time as you get used to this system of filing that you may want to make upgrades to your system at the start of each year. This is something you can look forward to. I like to refer my clients to the best person I know to help them in the area of technology and creating systems to keep organized on their electronic devices.

Getting back to your binder, you are going to use it as a way to keep track of all or most expenses you have on a daily basis to help you keep on top of your spending habits, to store bills you paid, to organize mail from the week you still need to go through, for other things you may need to refer to such as notes from your children's school, and more.

The plastic page protectors are to keep all papers neatly organized in categories. Use the sticky tabs to label each one. You can use the slide lock binder pouches if you want the more expensive option. Further down below are some examples of categories you may choose to store your papers in. What I like about the pouches is that they save you from having to punch out three holes in each paper that you are storing and are great for storing small papers like receipts. All you have to do is slip the paper inside the pouch and you are done! I also prefer to keep these papers in a binder rather than in a filing box so that it can be kept in a convenient location for you to access on a regular basis and you can take it wherever you go easily (as you may even want to sort through some things if you arrive early for an appointment for example).

In the front of the binder you will place a piece of blank paper. As you file each bill, receipt or other item into one of the plastic pouches in the binder, decide if you need to keep track of the expense. If you do, track this on the paper at the front. Create columns for the different expenses you have and immediately write them down (yes...hand write instead of going to your electronic device if you prefer to do it the old fashioned way).

You will be using this binder for one year's worth of papers so at the end of the year you will have tracked all of your expenses for your personal use, tax purposes and it will be very easy to get your totals for each column. When the year is over place your beautiful binder in the "Bin for Tax Purposes" (that I describe later on). The following year start with a fresh binder with fresh energy. Just remove any items from the previous year's binder that you still need, and transfer them to their new living space.

Below is a sample list of categories to help you create plastic pouch homes for your papers. Remember that you can come up with your own creative names too (as I described earlier).

- cell phone and land line
- water, gas, electricity
- car maintenance
- gasoline
- groceries
- health (such as prescriptions, medical/dental expenses not covered by insurance)
- personal (things you bought for your home, clothing, sports equipment, etc.)
- business associations/certifications
- extracurricular activities and courses
- children's school information/calendar
- carpool list
- rental agreement

You can use the business card holder pages to store the smaller items that you feel you may want inside your binder. Some things to store inside may be:

- stamps
- extra keys (put a piece of masking tape on each key and label what it is for)
- business cards from those you need to connect with, or have to enter their information still in your electronic contacts
- loose buttons that you plan to sew back on your clothing

You will find space in my free workbook that you can download at www.divinedeclutteringbook.com to create your own list so that you will know how many page protectors, etc. you will need to purchase.

All unopened mail will be stored in a binder pocket at the front or in a slide lock binder pouch if you prefer. Your new home for unopened mail will now be inside the binder. There is no need for you to come home and find mail sitting on countertops or at your front door and then experience the feelings that come up connected to the envelopes. Most likely they create more stress in you than anything, so it is better that the mail is put away until the time you are ready to deal with it.

I also love to empty my purse of loose papers with my binder next to me. It is my regular practice to do this every evening and it is so automatic that I do it with such ease now just like brushing my teeth. It will be important to figure out what time is best for you to sort through your mail and get your items into the binder. I like to go through my mail on Fridays so that I feel relaxed going into the weekend. I like to put everything else in my binder as the papers come in, such as receipts from purchases, on a daily basis. See what works best for you and make it a regular practice.

3. Bin For Tax Purposes

Where I live, residents have to keep documents for tax purposes for seven years so I have a bin large enough to hold seven years worth of papers. I keep the bin in a location that is out of the way. Find out how long you need to keep your papers for and then purchase a bin for them. I recommend using a clear plastic container so that you can see what is inside and will save you from having to label it. I also suggest using plastic instead of a cardboard box as it is waterproof and will protect your pages from water damage or bugs. Bugs can easily crawl into the layers of the cardboard and make their home there. Also, the overall structure of the box can become flimsy over time as you handle it and with the varying temperatures in your home, so get the plastic bin. You will always have enough room inside if you commit to removing the oldest year's paperwork as the newest year's papers go in. Shred the old immediately. Let it all go.

4. Binder For Recipes

Everyone in my family loves to cook and bake and so we have a lot of recipes and are always adding to our collection. We love finding new recipes on the internet and saving them in a folder on our computer, and also choose to print some out. I like to use the same "Peace Of

Mind Binder" concept for the recipes that I print out. I have one binder filled with plastic page protectors and slide each recipe into a pocket. I use the sticky labels to keep the pages in categories...appetizers, salads, meats, soups, dressings, desserts, etc.

When I am ready to use a recipe I take the page it is on out of the binder and when done I put it back. The page will always stay clean as the plastic can be easily wiped from what may spill onto it as you are busy creating something delicious. If you have recipes stored on small cards, find a nice box and store them in there, also creating categories. There are so many wonderful recipe sorting systems you can purchase. I have given you the simplest and least expensive option. It works.

5. Back Of Cupboard

I do not like to use my fridge as a display board. I find it looks messy and prefer to keep it clear of clutter as much as possible. Right now I only have a couple things posted on one side of my fridge. I keep a list of emergency phone numbers which is important to have for my children, and a couple papers from important events coming up because I like the feeling that thinking about them creates inside of me. One of the papers has to do with getting my book done so I like to always pass by this notice as it motivates me to write!

For other information I may need in a moment's notice, I use the back of one kitchen cupboard door, and only one. By using the inside of a door your kitchen will look neater and the papers will not take up precious space on your counter surfaces. I recommend to not use more than one or two inside cupboard door surfaces or it will just feel like more clutter. Some things that you may want to place on there are the school calendar, rules for recycling in your area, important information to remember about your pet such as a list of foods that are dangerous for them to ingest, invitations to events, or anything else that you feel would be good to post instead of storing in your "Peace Of Mind Binder."

A great idea is to stick a plastic pouch or envelope on the inside of the door to be able to place things inside such as party invitations. You will know when the party is taking place as you will have the date marked in your calendar, being the very organized "Queen" you are. When the party is done, recycle the invitation. You may even decide that when the invitation arrives and after you immediately mark the date in your calendar along with all other important details, that you toss the invitation at that point. I like keeping the invitations until the party. You do what feels best to you.

6. Baggie For Coupons

I find that the simplest way to keep coupons is in a zip lock bag or envelope. I do not like to keep the whole coupon collection in my wallet or purse as they take up too much space. What I do is keep the bag of coupons in the glove compartment of my car because I drive to most places I shop at so this is convenient for me. Then I just take out the coupon I know I will use that day or take the whole little bag into the store with me and pull out what I need. If I receive a coupon in the mail and know that I have to get it into my bag that is in the car, I just put it on top of my purse so that the next time I go out I will know to get it into its proper home in the car.

If you don't have a car, and either walk or use public transportation to get around, then you may want to tape an envelope to the inside of one of your kitchen cupboard doors, keep the coupons in there and then pull out the ones you will need that day before you go to the store. I always plan what I want to purchase before going into a store and create a shopping list if I need more than a little handful of items. Planning on what I want to purchase before shopping helps me stay on budget, and making a list on my phone or on a piece of paper of what I am going to buy, instead of having to remember everything clears up space in my mind.

I also find that when I have a shopping list and go to the store with my children, I feel calm. They know that I will only buy what is on the list, and this stops them from whining about something they may want that they see as we walk through the aisles. Sometimes as a treat I will pick up something they notice, however before going to the store I ask them what they would like, so they do have a say and they do get what they ask for. If there is something else they want and I do not pick it up as a treat that day, I tell them that we can get it next time. I feel it is important to teach children to sometimes wait for what they want and to also teach them the importance of budgeting. They also are aware of healthy eating habits so know not to ask for too much of the "junk food" items.

7. Bin For Children

I love to keep my children's artwork, projects and other things they create or receive such as small medals and trophies. I think it is wonderful to have a collection for them to keep as a memory of their childhood and so I do my best to keep those special items neatly organized until they are old enough to decide what they want to do with them. I choose only a few things (as far as artwork and things they write such as short stories) from each year to keep and get rid of the rest.

For important papers such as report cards, letters they receive to acknowledge something important they did and award certificates, I suggest keeping them in the filing drawer you created. Then it is very easy to hand over this file to your children when they are older and ready to move into their own place. I store everything else they create on paper, in one of two bins. I have one large clear plastic bin to keep pieces of artwork, projects or anything else they did or received such as a medal or ribbon that they feel they want to keep, and one clear plastic bin the size of a filing box that holds some school work from the year before, in case they want to refer to something from the past year. I then shred everything in that bin once they get to the next year, so the papers in there move through a yearly cycle.

Choose whatever size bin fits best in your storage area for your children's artwork and other memorabilia. I keep the bins for my children all in the same storage area. The art bin for each of my daughters is rectangular and large so that larger pieces of paper can fit nicely inside. I choose not to keep these bins in their rooms because I like to only have things in their room that they use regularly.

When an art project comes home, I put it on display for a while and then decide whether to keep it or throw it out as the next piece of art comes in. If it is a keeper, I put the date on the back and sometimes a little note about the piece, then it goes directly into the bin. I just take a nice walk to the location of the bin, use that time to connect to how much I love my children, pop the lid off the bin and put the item inside. I do not pile other bins on top of this one because if I did, I know I would wait and store the item at another time. This causes more clutter to build in my home, so I make sure that the bin is easily accessible, just out of the way.

Something else you may want to do is take pictures of the favorite pieces of artwork instead of holding onto them. You can later create a beautiful book online of all of your children's creations. This is a great idea to do for larger art and science projects that are just too bulky to store. One of my grandfathers loved to paint and create gorgeous things from stained glass. His pieces were displayed throughout his home. One of my cousins spent a lot of time taking pictures of every painting our grandfather painted and every stained glass piece he created and then made a book online using every picture. It is so wonderful to have this as a memory of him and his amazing priceless pieces of art. There were books made for every member of our family so we each have one to enjoy. I appreciate what she did for us so much!

I have a bin for myself that holds special things from my childhood. I enjoy having this to show to my children and it also brings back wonderful memories as I go through what is inside. I have removed some of the items from my collection over the years. I just keep checking in with my inner "Queen" and follow what this inner voice expresses to me. Do what feels best to you and just stay aware of the space you have for storage. Only keep things if you have a place for them.

8. Bookshelf For Reading Material

As books and magazines are made from paper they will be discussed in this section. My simple recommendation is to keep all reading material in one place. If you have children however, you will probably want to separate their books from yours. If there is room in their bedrooms you can keep their books in there so that they can easily select what to read or have you read to them at bedtime. If there is not enough room to keep all books in the bedroom, store their collection in the area of the home where you keep their toys.

As far as your books, only keep those that are your favorites that you know you like to refer to sometimes and align with who you are. Let go of the rest; give them away and let others enjoy them. Decide on the location you want to keep your books, go through the enjoyable process of making that area sacred first as I discussed earlier, and then go through your home to collect the books. I like to keep my books in a closed cabinet so that they do not collect dust. This cabinet happens to be in my basement. I enjoy bringing my friends and family down to the bookshelves to view my collection and to share with them those books that catch their attention. As much as I adore books, I am ok with keeping them out of the way of the main traffic areas and activity in my home. If I had a room set up to be my library or a section of my home that had an entire wall designed to be a bookshelf, I would love to have my books in there but for now, I am content with the storage space I am using.

I just have one more comment and suggestion about book storage... I do not recommend keeping piles of books and magazines in your bedroom as it is important to keep your room as empty as possible so that you are able to hear your own voice during your sacred quiet resting time in there, instead of the voices of others that may be coming from the pages. Only keep next to your bed the one or few books you are actively reading and put the rest away on your book shelf.

If you have a collection of magazines and newspapers, commit to recycling them regularly. You can find all the information from old papers through the internet and you can easily rip out pages from the magazines of whatever it is you think is important for you to keep and place them in a file in your filing drawer. Remember though, you are to only have in your home things that align with what you want in your life and make you feel good, so be selective with what you choose to read and keep.

To make it easier for you to be able to let go of old magazines and books think of this... Imagine that you purchased a ticket to go to the movies or to the theatre to see a live show. You made the investment and then enjoyed the entertainment for about a couple of hours. When the show was done you left the theatre hopefully feeling great because you enjoyed the show. You got your money's worth, enjoyed the good feelings that lingered on for a while from the experience, then got excited thinking about what the next show you see may be. Think of this the next time you finish reading through a magazine you purchased. Think of that time as the show being over, know you got your money's worth and let it go. Give the magazine away to someone you know will enjoy it or do my favorite thing...leave it on a bench at the next place you visit such as the mall or bus stop so that someone you don't know receives a gift. Practice random acts of kindness.

You can also create a rule for yourself that states that you will keep all magazines for one month until the next issue comes out and then let the previous ones go. If you like to relax on the couch and glance through them for inspiration once in a while, then create a neat pile on your coffee table. If you enjoy reading while in the restroom, then keep a little collection in there too. Just remember to get rid of the old ones from there as you committed to doing monthly.

9. Bag For Recycling

As you are going through all the papers in your home and running into them as you declutter each space in each room, have available a bag or bin to toss the recycling into. If something needs to be shredded, then do it as soon as you can. I recommend that you purchase a shredder, if you don't already have one and use it as soon as you have something you need to shred. If you let papers pile up then this creates more clutter. If you have a huge amount of shredding material then consider hiring a company to do the shredding for you.

As far as getting the mail, when I take out mail from my mailbox, I take a moment and go through each peace and immediately put into the recycling bin everything that I do not need and then put the rest of the important mail into my "Peace Of Mind Binder" to go through at the time I have scheduled to do this. I keep the recycling bin in my garage which has a door into my home. I do not find it to be a big deal to take a little walk to get to it. I see movement as a positive thing. I see that taking a few extra seconds to remove papers/envelopes/flyers that I do not need from surfaces in my home as a good thing too. Doing this keeps my space clear of energy from items that are unnecessary to be lying around.

This practice also adds to taking care of my mind because instead of walking by the kitchen counter for example, which may be piled up with these papers and flyers, and feeling frustrated and stressed about the mess, I will walk by that clear counter and feel more at peace because it is empty.

Wherever you choose to keep your bag or bin for recycling, just make sure you commit to going to it regularly. Remember to use your feminine flowing walk as you take the recycling to its location instead of moving quickly and with tension. Feel good that you are protecting your home from clutter as you do this, and also doing something good energetically and for your mind.

You Will Only Show Your X-Rated Belongings When Necessary

I know that you have a lot of items sitting around your home, taking up space in all kinds of drawers and hiding in corners that really do not make any sense being there. These are items that have zero sentimental value, are not very pretty and have odd shapes. These are the X-tra things we tend to keep around "just in case" we need them some time. Can you think of what you may have in your home that you can label as X-rated? Your job will be to collect all of these items and then think of one location in your home to store them so that they are always going to be easy to find when needed. You often need these things in a hurry so I promise you that you will really enjoy the organizing system I will describe next, instead of wasting time running around your home and feeling naughtily disorganized as you search for what you need.

These are some of the X-Rated items I am talking about:

Batteries

Light bulbs

Masking tape, scotch tape, duct tape, packing tape

Extra wires for electronic devices

Instruction manuals for household items and electronics

Thank you cards/holiday cards

Gift bags/wrapping/ribbon

Candles/lighters

Locks for luggage/lockers

Extension cords

You will store all of these items and others that you find around your home and that you feel would fit on this list in a nice plastic drawer system, or several drawer units, depending on how much you have to put away. There is room to create your own list so that you will know how many drawers you will need in my free workbook that you can download at www.divinedeclutteringbook.com.

You don't X-pose the X-rated parts of you to just anyone who may enter your home do you? You keep those sacred parts of you private and probably only X-pose in the privacy of your bedroom. Use this thought as your inspiration to get those X-rated items into their new location!

You should store these drawers in your basement, utility room, garage, closet or wherever else you feel is out of the way yet easy to get to in a hurry, because sometimes you may need to get to something quickly. I suggest making a list of all the things you think you would want to store in this way, then go out and purchase the drawers, especially paying attention to the size of each one. You will need larger drawers for the more bulky objects such as light bulbs. These units usually come with drawers of two or three sizes in one, so select what would work best for your items.

In order to keep all of those extra cords for your electronic devices organized, put each one in a zip lock bag and label it, describing what that cord is used for. As far as the instruction manuals, you may have fewer to store than you think because most can probably be found online, so check what is and then only keep the manuals you cannot locate through a search. If you have a collection of tools, it is best to purchase a toolbox and keep everything in the category of tools inside that will fit. Some things you may store in there could be hammers, screw drivers, measuring tapes, nails and picture hanging supplies.

I suggest that taking action with your X-rated items in your home is a good place to begin your physical decluttering and organizing. Since you probably have no sentimental attachment to these things, if you find you have too many of something (such as light bulbs for example) it will hopefully be easy for you to get rid of the excess and be able to "let go" with ease.

You will probably also enjoy starting to go through your home and collecting those odds and ends before you get to the bigger job of decluttering rooms. It will just make your job of decluttering everything else a bit easier with those little things out of the way. Surrender to your inner "Queen" as you collect and sort through all of the items. Remember that it is better to store less than more, especially when many of the items can probably be purchased for very little cost at a dollar store when needed.

For example, if you find you have enough wrapping paper to fill four drawers up, then this is too much. Eliminate and fit everything into one drawer. Perhaps you will want one drawer for wrapping paper and tissue and a second drawer to store the gift bags and ribbon. You can label each drawer to make it really easy to find what you need, or you may not even need to since the drawers are clear plastic. If you can see what is inside, don't waste your time labelling.

IF you have extra office supplies such as pens, paperclips and little pads of paper, I suggest storing those in the drawers too so that you have more space open in your office area or at your desk. When you need something, you will know exactly where to go being the very organized woman you have become! You will enjoy your walk to the location, because walking is good for you and you can practice X-pressing from your feminine (for example you may choose to sing) as you do this and pick up what you need with a smile.

You Will Cherish Your Priceless Moments

I come from a family that loves to take photos. My parents have created many beautiful albums over the years and so have I. My mother used to run scrapbooking classes and I loved participating. I enjoyed designing each page the photos were on and then selecting which photos to keep. This was a good exercise for me because I learned that it is not necessary to have many pictures displaying the same people in different poses; and unnecessary to have many pictures of similar beautiful settings, such as an ocean sunset, if seeing only one or two of these pictures gives me the same good feeling effect as seeing all of them did. Therefore, if you have loose pictures that you need to sort through, keep this in mind when deciding what to keep and what to let go of. You also may have a relative that would want some of the family photos you plan on parting with so check with them first before you throw them away.

Loose photos should be stored in an acid free box. Whether you store photos in albums, boxes or electronically, keep them organized in one place. Create folders on your computer and store pictures grouped by the year, month, occasion or whatever way you choose. You want to think of a way to store them so that you can locate them easily when needed.

Find a location in your home that can hold the number of photo albums and/or boxes of photos and other special memorabilia you may have and keep everything there. Choose a place that is out of the way because these things are not what you use on a daily basis, yet keep them accessible. You want to save prime storage space for items you use regularly. If you want to enjoy time looking through some of your albums with your family or guests who come over, just go to their location and bring them out. Your guests will wait as you do this. It is not necessary to keep "family" albums in the "family" room or room you entertain in, if there is not enough space there and if they are not handled regularly. As far as camera equipment, if you have any, you may want to keep it all in the same location as your photos.

You Will Take Care Of Your C's (cell phone, computer, crafts)

I am going to discuss just briefly for this book three more things that you also should keep organized and clear from clutter. They are your cell phone, computer and collection of craft supplies. Make sure you remove from your cell phone all contacts you no longer need, and if you receive email on your phone and check messages throughout your day, immediate delete those messages you know you do not need. Do not let them pile up. Do the same thing when on your computer. As you check your emails delete as you go. To keep emails organized on your computer I recommend creating folders and once you have completed taking action on an email, get it into the correct folder if you need to save the email. I have the best technology expert who helps those clients of mine who need support organizing information on their electronic devices, so I will not be discussing anything further here, as it is not my area of expertise.

If you have young children I am sure you have a huge assortment of craft supplies and even if you don't have children in your home, you may have this for yourself to enjoy. My recommendation is to store everything in one location. I like using the tall plastic drawer units for my family's craft supplies and I keep the units in the same location as the X-rated items. I keep like items together and so when I need something such as paints or pads of sketching paper, I know they will all be in the same drawer so I just remove the drawer from the unit and take it to the location in my home the painting activity is being done in. For smaller items such as writing supplies, glue sticks, paint brushes, craft scissors, jars of sprinkles, buttons, feathers, stickers, etc., I like to use smaller drawer units. I keep the small craft supplies together in zip lock bags like the little jars of sprinkles and buttons and then place them in the drawers. You can also use a large bin instead of a drawer system to store all of these things if you feel you have too much for drawers or prefer that kind of shape of storage box.

Store crayons, markers, and pencil crayons in a smaller unit of drawers that can fit on a table top. When it is coloring time your children can take the whole unit to the place they are coloring and everything is at their fingertips. If you have a regular place in your home where the crafting takes place then store everything in that location as long as you have room. If you do not have room, know that it will be easy to pull out the drawers of things you need and carry them over to where the art activity is taking place.

Now that you have been X-posed to several suggestions on how to tackle some of the smaller pieces of physical clutter in your home that you may have scattered around, are you feeling more confident that you can get all items mentioned here in order and in an enjoyable way? I hope you are! Pay attention to what you bring to your life with each healthy change you make in your home. Stay present in your days to take notice and you will be amazed! Remember also to see the new storage areas you created as sacred. Take care of these spaces and respect the objects in them. Do your best to protect these divine nine districts from clutter.

I have some wonderful things to share with you on the remaining pages of this book including a really sexy thought I consider to be X-rated that is just up ahead! Whenever it is that you feel prepared to take that symbolic and confident step to begin to remove the rest of the clutter from each of your rooms and create more beautiful sacred spaces, the next chapter will be ready to receive you. If that time is now, then with your royal crown upon your head and your "My Life In Pictures" book in your hands, please go ahead and enter Chapter 10. Two of your greatest supports and guides (meaning your inner "Queen" and the Universe of course), are already there waiting for you...

CHAPTER 10
You Will Select A Location And Do As You Are Told

Welcome to the final chapter on clearing your clutter! This is the last chapter on the subject yet in no way the least important one. This is the place where I give you suggestions on how to release your physical clutter in the most elegantly graceful and simple steps, as you move from one location in a room to the next. So far, you have learned what to do to let go of some of your non-physical clutter which will affect how you *feel* as a result of doing that; and in the previous chapter I gave you a little bit of an experience of what it feels like to create *feel good* spaces through the designing of your personal sacred space. I then gave you suggestions on how to create new homes for some of your possessions that you may have had to search for from many different locations in your home (such as all your craft supplies for example and organize them by category).

In this chapter, you are going to learn how to let go of your physical clutter tackling one area at a time in each room to be able to *feel and see* the amazing, immediate results of your work quite quickly! You will take action to create sacred spaces in each room in the place of cluttered ones, choosing items to keep that aligned with your best self, what you want, what you find useful and what you imagine wanting to see in your "My Life In Pictures" book. Remember to ask yourself The Grand

Question, "Do I want this item to show up in my book?" This is the time where you will feel the joining of hands start to happen of each organized space as each is created, along with the magical support that this brings you.

Before you begin taking action, I'd like to share that sexy X-rated thought I mentioned at the end of the last chapter. I enjoy being creative and having fun as much as I can throughout my days no matter what I am doing, as I feel it is important to play in life and not always be so serious; so here is a little bit of playfulness for you...

The art of decluttering can be seen as a sensual and intimate activity and compared to the art of lovemaking. The more you get into the experience of connecting with and making love to your partner, I imagine the deeper you want to feel, know and receive pleasure from your love on all levels, and want more and more of this kind of experience together...correct? As you get into the experience of connecting with and being present with all of your possessions as you love yourself and see yourself as sacred in the process of decluttering, I hope you enjoy it so much that you have the desire to dig deeper and deeper into your piles, and feel how sensual, enjoyable and intimate of an experience this can be for you.

I hope that as you sink deeper into the experience and choose to only keep what you love, items that align with your best self and those you receive pleasure from, that you just want to do more. Make love to your "stuff" in your cluttered spaces. Move slowly, and be present as you declutter and give thanks to all items that served you well in your past. Once you release all that no longer belongs in your life from one area and then claim this space to be your sacred one, shout out in your most divinely feminine and fabulous voice, "YES!" You want your life to become one filled with lots of "YES's." Feel yourself saying "YES" to you, and create your life to be one where you only choose to do things, and have things in your life that you say a firm, grounded, freeing, powerful and oh so gratifying and satisfying "YES" to!

Feel your home as a gift box that contains everything precious and that is meaningful to your heart and soul. Declare this gift box to be your safe space for all you hold dear. Think of yourself as a gift box too...the safe space you create for your heart and soul's acceptance and expression with zero judgement attached. A little secret (while on the topic of intimacy with a partner) is that when you feel you hold a powerful safe space for your heart and soul's expression inside of you, and connect with yourself authentically, you allow your partner to feel that they can feel safe with you too, to express what is in their heart and soul. You will make no judgements, not criticize, not figure out how you want to fix your love, or correct what they are feeling as your partner expresses to you. All you need to do is allow your partner to be and to express; just as you allow yourself to do the same.

Presented here are the general guidelines I use for organizing and those my clients have enjoyed using too. From a very young age, I loved collecting things. I had collections of rocks that I tumbled in my rock tumbler, stickers, stationary, pressed leaves, little glass figurines and more. I stored each separate collection in a shoe or boot box, decorating the outside of each one with wrapping paper so that it looked pretty. I also made "rooms" out of boxes to display my rocks in, and glued down several in each box along with labels to identify each one. Each box became a room of my little museum.

When my friends came over with their collections, we often enjoyed trading our treasures and so it was very easy to just grab my box and have everything to show them at my fingertips. I did not have parts of a collection in one room and then other parts scattered in another location. I was very proud of what I owned and enjoyed keeping everything safe and in one place. I want you to think of this as you decide where and how you want to keep everything in your home.

You probably sensed that I like organizing in categories from what you learned in the previous chapter...so, my recommendation for items you store is that you keep all items that fall in one category together in one location. This means that all of your shoes and outerwear for the season will be found in one place, all socks, cooking utensils, purses, jewellery, DVDs, etc. By doing this, you will only have one place to look to find what you need instead of running around your home in a panic trying to locate something when in a rush. This is a terrific way to teach your children to keep organized too. When my girls are looking for something they need, they know exactly where to go to find it and it is always there. If a piece of clothing they are looking for is not in its place for example, then they know it is in the wash pile and nowhere else in our home.

Now that you have in mind as you declutter that it will be important to store by category, I want you to take a walk through your home and begin thinking of what you see being stored in each room. Think of keeping items that you use regularly in places that are easy to get to and make sense being there, and imagine storing the rest that you do not use as regularly in places that are more out of the way such as up high in a closet, a storage closet, basement, garage or attic. Do your best to get a general idea at this point. As you begin to declutter your first room, you will see that your inner "Queen" will guide you and help you decide what is best to keep in that space and in every piece of storage furniture, shelf and closet you have in there.

You will also find that as you move along, you will have an easier and easier time deciding where to keep things. You may also find that you decide on keeping a group of items in one location, and then change your mind and that is completely ok to do. There is no right or wrong way. You just have to make sure you feel good with your choices because your aim is to feel as best as possible in your home.

As you walk from room to room you may take notice of the place with the most clutter build-up. Think of why this may be. For example, if you have the most clutter and disorganization in your office space then perhaps there is something really bothering you related to what you do for a living. This outer clutter may be the tip of the iceberg of something inside that you could not see unless you make the choice to look in.

My last instruction before you begin is the following...you will declutter one section of a room at a time. For example, if you choose the dresser of several drawers in your bedroom to begin with, then you will need to decide first what items you want to have in the drawers and on the surface. Once you have a good idea of what you want to store and where, you will begin your decluttering. You will begin this task by clearing out everything from that location, cleaning the surfaces, doing whatever ritual you feel is best to remove the stagnant energy (as I suggested in the previous chapter as you created your personal sacred space) and then put back only what you want to keep.

If you find that something you pulled out, from the dresser for example, belongs in another room, then at the end of your decluttering session make sure you take that item to the place where it belongs. If you still haven't done your decluttering in the room that item is supposed to be in, then start a little pile and know that it will soon be placed in its home. I want you to feel ok with being in the state of "transition" as you declutter and reorganize your living space. Feel good about the little piles of things that you transported from another location that may build in each room, knowing that they will eventually have a home to live in. These piles will have a different energy from your piles of clutter...a good feeling energy. You will see. Unwanted items will either go in the garbage or in a bag to donate or sell.

Once you finish putting everything in order in your new sacred space, make the commitment that you will take care of this area and only bring things to that space that belong there, keeping all clutter out. Also, remember the letter from the objects in your space that I wrote about in Chapter Six. Give everything in your space a heartbeat and feel the loving support around you.

Some people feel uncomfortable with a lot of change and uncomfortable to be in a space that is not filled with an overflow of things, so by creating one sacred space at a time I am hoping that those of you who feel this way will be able to experience this new energy in a way that feels comfortable and safe for you. Over time I hope that you enjoy the feelings that your new clutter-free spaces bring you along with the changes in your everyday experiences that I am sure you will see too, as you start to feel better and better! I hope that this will drive you to keep going to create more and more beautiful spaces as you let the clutter go.

When in doubt about which area to declutter next, put your hand on your heart, close your eyes and ask your inner "Queen" your question. Then wait for the answer. Your answer may come immediately into your awareness or you may receive it as a "sign" as you are doing something else. For example, if you do not receive an answer right away and you go ahead with your day, perhaps it will be that when you open up a magazine the first thing you see is a dresser that looks like yours and all of a sudden you will just know that you need to declutter your dresser next; or perhaps an email will come in from your library reminding you of your overdue book and this may be your cue to declutter the area where you know you have a ton of books and old newspapers piled up. If you are ready for some divinely sacred and sensual sorting and releasing, please open the door to your beautiful home and step into your entranceway. Remember to bring with you all that you have learned in the previous chapters, along with your "My Life In Pictures" book. Connect with your divine feminine power and your dreams and let's begin...

In order for you to declutter and set up your spaces in as organized a fashion as possible, I will be providing most suggestions in point form so that you can take action moving from one suggestion to the next in any order that you like, checking off those you complete as you move along.

As each home is different, not all suggestions will apply to your living space so take what you feel will work for you, make modifications if needed and leave the rest. Also remember to use your inner "Queen's" guidance for other ideas. Below you will find just a few of mine that have worked for my clients. I really want you to start trusting your inner voice instead of relying on others to give you all of the answers. You have all answers inside of you...just listen. Decorating suggestions will not be provided in this chapter and will be covered in the last one in a very fun way! For now, focus on getting the clutter out and creating your sacred spaces.

Your Entranceway

Your home takes care of you and you now will be showing your appreciation and respect in return by taking care of it, in addition to creating it to be a place you love living in. Your front entranceway is the first place you see as you enter and so I suggest you begin to declutter there and claim it to be one of your newest sacred spaces. You deserve to feel good as soon as you enter your home and doing this will help. I know that you want new experiences, people and things to enter your life so make sure that you clear the way for this. If you want flow in your life then begin to create it right at your front door. Remove everything that blocks energy and people from easily entering inside and being able to gracefully move through to get to the connecting spaces. Below are some suggestions on what items to store and how to store them in this space including in the entrance closet (if you have one).

- Unless you have room in your entrance closet, store off season outerwear including footwear in another location that you designate for storage.
- If keeping off season items in your closet, put them in the hardest to reach areas until it is time to use them...then move them to the front and easy access places when needed again next year.

- Hang an organizing system in your closet that has clear plastic pockets to keep various small items that you may need to use or take with you as you go out the door. You will always know where to look for what you need by doing this. Store items such as sunglasses, swim goggles, sunscreen, a sticky roller to clean the lint off your coat, your keys, wallet, wipes made for cleaning salt stains from shoes and boots, shoe horn, bus tickets, and loose change. As soon as you come home, remember to put back those items that you took out before you left, such as your keys. You will no longer have to run around your home in a panic looking for them if you do this. If you do not have a closet, then keep items organized by the entrance in a decorative storage unit or piece of furniture such as a storage bench seat.

- Hang a long narrow storage unit with shelves in your closet for winter scarves, gloves, earmuffs, hats, fabric shopping bags and small umbrellas

- If not using a hanging storage system, use the top shelf to store baskets to separate the scarves, gloves, etc.

- If you have a door that opens into your closet instead of sliding doors, hang a shoe organizer on the inside of the door to keep slippers, flip flops and other shoes. Store remaining shoes and boots on the floor inside. Use a shelf system to take advantage of the space you have from the bottom of the coats to the floor. Remember to leave some space open for your guests and for something new.

- At the end of each season, before storing your items until needed again or moving them to the back of the closet, get rid of what you feel you will not wear next year. If you did not use it this season, then you will most likely not use it again the next so let it go. Make room for something new.

- Use sturdy hangers, all of the same style and color and make sure you have extras ones hanging right in the front to send out the message to the Universe that you are welcoming new people and experiences into your life. Make your guests feel welcomed by having those hangers ready for them.
- Use the top shelf to store bulkier items such as the one purse you are using (others will be stored in your bedroom) and larger sun hats that cannot be folded. You can also hang hats on nails on the inside walls of the closet if you have room to do this.

Below is a collection of affirmations you may find soothing to express out loud to help you in letting go as you declutter. Write down the ones you like and some of your own as you declutter each room in your home in my free workbook that you can download at www.divine declutteringbook.com.

I am not attached to my clutter. I am attached to self-love and respect, serenity and peace.
There is no need to fear, because I trust divine support is here.
I let go and let go(o)dness come into my life.
To allow myself to grow, I am learning to let go.
I choose to stop my whining and trust in divine timing.
For a fresh start, I trust the voice in my heart.

I am the "Queen" of my life and love the entrance to my "Queendom."
The entrance of my home loves to receive me feeling at my best.

Your Bathroom

As the bathroom is quite a small area compared to your other rooms, I suggest that you complete your decluttering in here in one day and then be done with it. It will give you a feeling of great satisfaction knowing that you cleared one entire room of clutter in a short amount of time, and will be your inspiration to get moving in the rest of your home! Take everything out of the drawers, cupboards and off the counter and put everything together to start sorting through.

As you choose what you are going to keep, start grouping items that go together by category but do not put anything away yet. Do this on the floor or another place you choose to sort. That day or the next, purchase the storage units you would like (if you need any) that will fit all of your items that you now have to keep. Next, put everything neatly away in your sacred bathroom spaces. If you already have purchased storage units or have what you need at home, then do everything in one day.

- Get rid of items that are past the expiry date.
- Collect all first aid items and medicines that may be needed but not used regularly and store them together in a three-drawer unit. The first drawer will hold bandages and disinfectants, adult medications in the second and children's medicines and a thermometer in the

last if you have children. Store this unit out of the bathroom as you will not be using the items daily, and if you have place somewhere else near your bedrooms. I suggest a high shelf in the linen closet. You want to keep all medicines out of sight and not at eye level because when you see them, it may trigger thoughts of illness and instead, you want thoughts of health.

- Keep medications you use regularly away from eye level storage locations such as the medicine cabinet (especially if you open that door regularly) so that you are not regularly reminded of health issues. As you clear your inner and outer home from clutter you may notice that your health improves as everything is connected. I travelled to the U.S. to help declutter a very old apartment space that was owned by a well-known gentleman who had a successful business where he worked with many celebrity clients. His business however, started to suffer as he had an injury and then had a hard time getting off the pain medications he was on. As I removed the clutter over a period of time, and his possessions were organized in a way that suited him, including in his home office space, he started feeling better and better. His doctor was shocked that over a few short weeks he had cut his doses by a large amount, when prior to the decluttering he had the most difficult time reducing what he took even slightly. Decluttering was good for his health.

- Keep like items together such as all lipsticks, nail polishes, eye shadows, etc. and then ask your inner "Queen" the best way to store them. If you need to keep some things on the counter due to lack of other storage space, place them in a storage/makeup display unit that is easy to lift off the counter in order to be able to clean the surface when done getting ready each morning.

- Keep feminine paper products in a storage basket instead of in the packages they come in to see your supply easily. Move them to the back of the cupboard when not in use.

- Assign no more than four towels per person and a few wash cloths. For a spa-like feel hang a shelf designed to hold towels and store what you can there. You can also roll them up to be on display in a decorative basket or keep them piled neatly at the side of the tub or on another surface you may have available. Towels can also be hung from a rack or hooks on the door. If there is no room to store extra towels in your bathroom, then keep them in the linen closet. You may also want to use your linen closet to store bathroom items that you do not use regularly and for extra supplies you purchased. Keep like items together in storage baskets.

- If you want to be in a relationship then make sure to create open spaces in your bathroom storage areas and on the counter to send out a message to the Universe that you are ready to welcome your partner into your life.

- Keep extra toilet paper rolls in every bathroom of your home. Either store them stacked in the cupboard, in a decorative basket if on display or in something that is specifically designed to hold the rolls. You do not need to purchase more packages of rolls than what you can fit in your bathroom even if they are on sale at the store, as they are always going on sale. You will have enough of a supply at home if you do as I recommended. When you see that the supply is getting low in a bathroom, just remember to add this item to your shopping list for your next trip.

- Collect hair off the floor after getting ready in the morning and any time you brush it because a "Queen" should not be walking on surfaces that are anything but clean and clear. This task takes a few seconds to do. I use a tissue to collect the hair and wipe the entire floor clean. It also gives me the opportunity to bend and do a nice stretch first thing in the morning. Make sure you wipe off the sink and countertop too so that they look clean the next time you go in.

Everything in this space serves a purpose related to my cleansing, reflecting and pampering.

As I wash my hands I remember to take care of myself first before doing for others.

As I shower, I allow the Universe to shower me with love and support.

As I brush my teeth I feel that those words that do not serve me well get washed away.

As I use the facilities I remember to release all that holds me back from feeling joyful.

As I apply my make-up I remember that I may be able to "cover-up" what I truly feel and need in my life, but I know that this does not serve me well. I am ready to look at, unconditionally love and pay attention to what is underneath.

As I remove my clothes and expose my naked body, I remember to practice detachment to all people, places and things.

Vulnerability is sexy.

Being vulnerable is part of being authentic and I am authentic.
Self-care is my divine responsibility.
I feel like a Queen with this space sparkling clean.

Your Bedroom

Create your bedroom to be your sanctuary, a place to receive inspirations from source and as a sacred space for intimacy. Have only items in there that you love and bring out feelings of love, romance and relaxation. You can improve your relationship with your partner by removing the television, photographs of anyone but the two of you, and everything that is connected to any other part of your day such as the mail and other papers, children's toys and dirty clothing.

I suggest keeping a laundry basket in the area you do laundry instead of in the bedrooms. Take a nice leisurely walk to that location every night and place your clothing in there. Teach your children to do the same. I also like to keep all shoes out of the bedroom closet as I prefer not to feel the energy near where I sleep that may be on the soles from other places. If you have room, find another location in your home to keep them. Your inner "Queen" knows where that best place is. Just remember to keep all shoes together. You may have some shoes that you wear almost daily so keep those in your front entrance closet. For those shoes you wear less frequently and for special occasions, store in the other location you have chosen.

When choosing how to fold and organize clothing in each drawer, do what feels best for you. I opened up one drawer in each of my daughter's dressers just before writing this paragraph, to see how they keep their clothing organized. I taught them from a very young age to be responsible for their clean clothing so they have been folding their own clothes and putting them away for a very long time. I also allowed them to figure out how to fold each item. I did not want to teach them and instead wanted them to use their own creative minds for this.

After opening each of their top drawers just a moment ago I must say that I am quite impressed! One of my daughters has her undergarments and bras in that drawer and it looks like the drawer came out of a lingerie shop. The bras are not folded, but lying flat and fanned to the back so she can see each one nicely. Each undergarment is rolled up individually into a pretty package and sorted into rows.

My other daughter did something different. She found a plastic bin that fits perfectly into one side of the drawer and this holds all of her socks. Each pair is rolled up into a ball. Undergarments are altogether next to the box (and not folded). Next to those is a neat small pile of her pajamas. She only has about four sets of pyjamas and when one becomes worn out, she gets excited knowing that she will get a new one to replace it.

I do not have a dresser in my bedroom and keep all clothing in my closet and in an armoire so my children did not learn from me how to organize a large dresser drawer. I decided to take a look into one more drawer for each of my girls so I opened the drawer just beneath the first one. My daughter who has the lingerie-shop-designed-drawer has all her t-shirts and tank tops in the next one. I was again quite impressed. She has all items folded in a way that allows them to stand on end and she created rows so you can clearly see all shirts as you open the drawer.

My other daughter did something different. She also has shirts stored in her next drawer but organized into neat piles separating short sleeved tops from long sleeved ones and tank tops. She stores items one on top of another. Do what feels best for you just as my daughters did for them. When ready, ask your inner "Queen" which area you should declutter first then start there. It may be your dresser drawers, night stand, surface of your bed, one side of your closet or the pile in the corner. Begin by creating one sacred space. Then when ready, move on to create another and then more until your entire room feels like the biggest gift of a peaceful safe space for you to relax and sleep soundly in, and also for enjoying sacred intimacy.

I have found that every client of mine so far likes to keep their clothing stored in a different way. I also found that for women who work outside of the home and have a collection of "office attire," some of them want to keep their clothing organized in a different way from those women who don't have clothing labeled as such. This makes it very difficult for me to know what to recommend to you so I will just give you the details of what I do as I do work from home sometimes, work outside of my home sometimes and am a stay at home mom for a good part of each year too. I am a little bit of every kind of woman so I hope that what I suggest here will help you.

All I have in the master bedroom is a bed, two nightstands, couch, decorative wooden unit to display things that I love and an armoire. I have some of my clothing in the armoire and everything else is stored in the walk-in closet. It feels peaceful and relaxing to me to come into a space that is not cluttered with a lot of objects on surfaces. There is a lamp on each night stand along with candles; and on my side I also have a pen and neat pile of some things such as my journal and the book I am reading.

I only use a little more than half of the closet for my clothing. The other part is the "his" side. My personal belongings stay in their designated "hers" sacred spaces. If you are not yet in a relationship and want to be, then you may want to create empty spaces for your future partner's items to go into so that the Universe knows you are ready for this (even if you picture the two of you living somewhere else). Be thoughtful and leave a generous amount of room for your future partner's items. By making the decision that you will not move into your partner's space, you are showing respect for this person on an energetic level. This will also help keep the amount of clothing you own down and force you to get rid of old items as you purchase new ones.

I believe that we are always provided with what we need when we need it, including enough storage space. With this belief, I feel that there is no need to store away out of season clothing outside of your bedroom. If you have a small closet, then perhaps it is a message that you need to cut down on what you have for this time in your life.

Below you will find my suggestions based on how I store my clothing and other items in the bedroom. Use your inner "Queen's" guidance as you stay connected to your feminine radiance and enjoy coming up with ideas for you to try! If you store your clothing one way for a while and do not like it, then try doing something else. You may also like changing the way you store and organize your clothing every few months, just to move the energy around a little, if you want some new movement to happen in your life!

When you are ready to declutter your closet but feel the entire space is too overwhelming to complete at once, then choose one section to work through at a time. Remove everything from that area, claim that space as your sacred one where clutter is no longer welcome and then only put back what you love and want to keep. Think of what you'd want to see show up in your "My Life In Pictures" book. Remember that you are only keeping things that align with your best self. Do not worry yet about organizing the closet. First just get the clutter out. Remove the clutter one section at a time until it is all out from the closet. At that point you can go ahead and arrange the clothing in the way that feels best to you.

Remember that once you finish decluttering an area, see how it makes you feel. Leave the room and then come in again and return to the area you just worked on and listen to your body. Perhaps there is still something in that space that needs to go if you don't have the urge to say "ahhhhhhh" and "YES!" as you look there.

- Decide on the place where you want your invisible (or real crown) to rest each night and create that space to be sacred. Do this first before anything else. Remove all clutter from the area and claim this space as your royal one. Place something decorative there to remind you that you are a divine Goddess and to hold the space for your crown while it is on your head. Also remember, that as a "Queen" you will connect to both your divine masculine and divine feminine in order to get your clutter out.
- Keep all hangers the same color and style for a calming feel.
- Hang clothing by category (i.e. all blouses together, pants, dresses, etc.). If you have some blouses that you wear as "office attire" and some that are not, then you may want to keep them in two separate groups yet still hanging next to each other so that it is easy in the morning to find what you need. You can do the same for your pants, dresses, etc. I keep like colors in each grouping together and play with the collection until I feel really good when I look at it. I keep outfits for special occasions in the part of my closet that is closest to the back with one exception... I love to feel myself getting dressed up to be taken out for a romantic evening and so I keep my most favorite dress right in the front of my closet so that when I walk in,

I see it first, along with some of my other most favorite pieces of clothing that connect me with some of my dreams. I love to spend time by the ocean and in warm climate so I also display my favorite sun dresses right in the front. I am interested in staying connected to what feels best to my heart, body and soul and being in summer clothing by the water feels that way, so this is the clothing that is featured in my closet. The ocean is soothing for my spirit. When I open the door I get a little bit of beach feeling energy and bright colors greeting me, even in the midst of Canada's coldest time of the year when temperatures go below freezing.

This is a neat story... many years ago, I chose to keep a beautiful handmade designer dress (eggplant in color with fine needlepoint decorative swirls throughout in the same color), right in the front of my closet because I enjoyed looking at it and also expected to one day be in a relationship with someone who liked to dress up once in a while and take me out for a nice evening. Can you believe that shortly after, a man that unexpectedly showed up in my life and I had developed a friendship with and then started dating, gave me a gift on our second meeting and it was a dress that was almost identical to the one in my closet?! I thought this was really odd as I was not expecting a gift and he knew nothing about my clothing. The dress was the same color, same full length, almost identical style with almost the same finely sewn pattern going through it. The only difference was that my dress was suitable for an elegant event and the one he gave to me was more casual that I could wear any time, and it fit me perfectly.

As much as I enjoyed wearing my new dress, I decided that when our relationship came to a close, that it was time to let the dress go too. I actually let both of the dresses go and felt thankful for the wonderful times I had in my past. What you place in your closet and what you think about matters.

If you think that this dress story may just be a coincidence, then let me give you one more story. I also had on display in one of my sacred spaces, a picture of my late grandfather (my mom's father) sitting on a horse wearing his soldier uniform in a forest in Poland. I loved remembering my grandfather and his nature, so I displayed his photo. The gentleman who unexpectedly showed up in my life, that I described above, had first sent me a photo of himself before meeting. The photo I received from him was almost identical to the one of my grandfather, except this gentleman was sitting on a motorcycle instead of on a horse. He was also wearing a soldier uniform. It shocked me! He told me that the photo was taken a few years earlier while he was in Iraq, and that he was a U.S. Army Captain/war veteran in the process of leaving the army. I had never met an American or Canadian soldier before. What are the chances of a meeting like this to happen for a woman living in a basement apartment in a quiet suburb of Ontario, Canada, focusing on her own life and not even on a dating site?! I have many stories like this one and it makes life feel so beautiful. Everyone and everything is connected.

Getting back to the dresses, instead of selecting another couple of dresses to put in their place in my closet, I decided to leave the space open and set an intention instead, then let my wish go. I can't even remember what I wished for at the time which is a sign that I really did let it go! I trust that I will recall what it was at the perfect time.

- You may want to change the organization of your clothing as the seasons change. I keep sweaters in my armoire. As I do not like to be reminded of the cold winter when it is not winter, I remove the winter sweaters from there when spring arrives and store them on a high shelf in a part of my closet I cannot see when I walk in. Before I store them however, I remove those sweaters I know I will not want to wear next year. I put them in a bag and donate. It does not matter to me that a sweater may still be in perfect condition or that I spent a fortune on that item. If it does not feel like it belongs in my life, then I remind myself that I got some good use out of it already and it is time that it goes.
- Keep all hanging blouses, dresses, jackets, etc. facing the same direction.
- You may like hanging clothing in your closet based on their weight, going from lightweight to heavyweight. You can begin on the left and start hanging all the lightweight blouses, then next to those are heavier tops, sweaters that need to be hung instead of folded, then pants, dresses next, then blazers and heavier items such as winter vests. Outfits for special occasions that are infrequently worn can be hung right at the end. If you have some pants such as jeans and

leggings that you prefer to fold instead of hang, then place them on the shelf just above where your pants are hung so they are altogether.

- Keep purses neatly displayed on a shelf in your closet. Take advantage of vertical space and put up more shelving if you can in order to have more room to store your items. You can store one purse in the next to save on space however I like to keep mine all on display, standing vertically and arranged by color. To make it easy to move everything from the inside of one purse to the next, I suggest purchasing a purse organizer. This will keep everything neatly together and will also help keep the inside lining of all your purses clean.

- Store smaller items such as bras, socks, undergarments and slips in your closet using a plastic drawer unit if you do not have space anywhere else in your room for them such as in a dresser.

- Think of how many pairs of socks you wear over two weeks or the time period in between doing the wash and keep that many. Get rid of the rest.

- Store nylons in a hanging organizer with clear plastic pockets and keep it in your closet. Store one pair of nylons in each pouch and get rid of those that are torn.

- Keep costume jewellery that you prefer not to be on display in a decorative way, in a hanging organizer designed for jewellery. It is best to get one that has pockets that zip closed so that small items like earrings do not fall out. Hang this in your closet. If you have jewellery that tarnishes like sterling silver, it is worth purchasing a similar kind of organizer but one that is lined with tarnish preventing silversmiths' cloth. A "Queen" only wears pieces that sparkle and are bright, just like her energy so this organizer will keep your jewellery looking that way. If you want to save time on polishing your pieces before wearing them, I recommend you make the investment and purchase this. You are worth it! As a less expensive option, keep your jewellery looking bright by storing it in small zip lock bags with the air removed. Keep larger sized necklaces that do not fit into an organizer on the same hangers that are holding the clothing you wear them with, such as a blouse or dress. Put each necklace (with matching bracelet, earrings, ring, broach if you have a set) in a large zip lock bag, punch a hole through the top and then place the hanger through the hole so that the bag rests on the front of the clothing. If you prefer not to make a hole in the bag, create a loop with ribbon and staple the ribbon to the top of the bag and let the ribbon hang from the hanger instead. Keep all other valuable jewellery in a place that makes sense to you.

- Create extra shelving in your closet by hanging a shelf system that closes with a zipper in order to keep dust out. It also keeps that area looking neat and tidy when it is closed. Store tank tops, t-shirts, workout clothing, bathing suits in this system.

- Store scarves on a hanger designed to hold them or in a basket. Keep belts the same way.

- Use a small area in your closet to display some of your favorite things and decorative items that connect you to your dreams so you receive a real treat as you open the door.

- Keep only what you love and what is in good condition and get rid of the rest. Remember your rules about how you will decide what to keep along with how many items from each category.

- Create empty spaces in your closet and drawers to welcome new things.

- Keep the area next to your bed as empty as possible so you have zero distractions around you from getting a good night's sleep.

- Clear off all surfaces and put all clothing and other items where they belong before you go to bed to send out a message to the Universe that you are ready to receive something new the next day and begin the morning feeling fresh. By not putting things away from the day before, you are bringing that old energy into the next day.

- Remove all electronic devices from this space as they can affect your quality of sleep. Use a battery operated alarm clock instead of the alarm on your phone so that you can keep your phone away from the bed. You may find that you get a better sleep the less you have plugged into outlets around your bed, and the further away your cell phone is from where you sleep. Keep the energy in your space clean and clear.

- Make your bed every morning and store two extra sheet sets in your linen closet. Treat yourself to luxurious sheets and a pretty duvet set so that your bed can take care of you in the best way as you sleep. You my Goddess, need a beautiful space for rest and rejuvenation. Sleep in a bed that feels royal and divine to you.

I love everything I wear and my clothing feels beautiful on my body.

I have my own unique style and this shines through by what I choose to wear.

All clothing I own has a fresh and clutter-free space to live in.

I am a divine and valuable woman, and remember this as I put my crown on each morning.

I always have room in my closet to receive new things.

What I wear reflects my feminine flare.

I slide between my fresh sheets feeling that I've surrendered. I am ok with the unknown and feeling the uncertainty for what is to come. I know all is perfect.

My blanket provides protection and reminds me of how my inner guidance protects and takes care of me.

To be at my best, I allow myself a good rest.

I make my bed each morning as a thank you for taking care of me through the night.

My thought as I rest, is that for today I did my best.

As hard as it sometimes seems, I continue to believe in all of my dreams.

I experience all feelings of unconditional self-love, authenticity, vulnerability, connection to the divine, sensuality, sexuality, romance, exquisite self-care and pleasure, and hot steamy fun in this sacred private space.

Once you finish removing the clutter and creating sacred organized spaces in your bedroom, I know that you will be very well prepared to continue doing the same in the rest of the bedrooms in your home.

Therefore, I am not providing suggestions on what to do in those ones. I want you to feel empowered and take the opportunity to do what feels best to you without me giving you tips. You can do it! It is also a good idea to get your kids involved when it is time to declutter their rooms. Teach them the importance of keeping organized and getting excited about giving away what they no longer use, as a gift to other children.

Your Kitchen And Dining Areas

Now that you know what to do with all of your loose papers, mail and coupons (which was described in the previous chapter) that most likely land in your kitchen area, you can easily put them all away. Once that is done, all that will be left in your kitchen to do is decide on how to best keep your dishes, silverware, items for entertaining, small appliances, cooking utensils, pots, pans and food items. Before you choose an area to begin to declutter, take a look around your kitchen and plan what you want to keep in each storage space. Ask your inner "Queen" for guidance. You want to keep things that you use regularly in convenient, easy to reach locations and items that are used less frequently in places that are harder to reach.

I enjoy entertaining and so I have many larger sized serving platters and extra sets of silverware. I do not have space in my kitchen to keep it all so I have chosen my cold cellar as my storage space for everything related to entertaining and cooking big meals (such as large soup pots). My children love baking and cake decorating and so we also have in the cold cellar the equipment they use for this. Everything is stored neatly on shelves and in baskets to group like items together such as small cake decorating supplies.

I do not mind that I have to take a walk down to the basement to retrieve what I need. Movement is good and I do not believe that everything has to be at fingertip length away, especially when not used regularly. I have never heard my children complain about having to go downstairs either. I think they find it to be a treat whenever they enter the cold cellar as they know that most things in there are connected to having fun and company over. I also chose this space to keep all tablecloths because they go under the category of entertaining.

Here are some suggestions on how to break down the kitchen and dining areas into sections to declutter, to be able to clean out one section at a time: fridge, freezer, all drawers at once, entire pantry, two cupboards at a time, area under the sink, spices organization, the entire surface of the table you dine on, all countertops at once.

- Keep your countertops as empty as possible which will help you feel calm.
- Place on countertops only those small appliances that you regularly use such as a coffee maker, toaster, blender and food processor. Store the rest in a cupboard, keeping all small appliances in the same location.
- Always wash pots, pans and utensils you use while cooking as you

go. Wash all dishes by hand or put them in the dishwasher right after each meal. Do not let them pile up to wash at the end of the day. If you do not have time to do this after each meal then perhaps you have to look at why. Eating in a relaxed way and keeping your kitchen clean is an important part of self-care. If it is important to you, you will adjust your schedule to honor this, period.

My children know that we do not leave the house until the kitchen is clean. They also are responsible to wash their own storage items from their school lunch bags including their water bottles. They know that the first thing they do when they get home is to hand wash those items and put their lunch bags away. When their containers are dry I put them back in their designated spaces or reuse them that evening to hold their lunches that I prepare for them for the next day. You need very few storage containers for lunches if you wash them daily, so decide on what your children need to use for the various lunches you pack them and then get rid of the rest. When one of them gets worn out, throw it out and purchase a new one.

- Always end your day with a sparkling clean and empty sink looking up at you. Put all clean dishes away that had been drying on the counter and from the dishwasher. When you choose to run your dishwasher after dinner, you have the opportunity to put the clean dishes away before you go to bed. Your morning will flow more smoothly if you don't have to do the unloading at breakfast time. All you will have to do is put your breakfast dishes in.

- Group items by category so keep all silverware together, dishes, cups, glasses, etc. Keep what you use regularly in convenient storage locations. If you have a large variety of mugs that do not match or many sets of silverware, you must ask your inner "Queen" for guidance. Think of how many mugs you use in one day and how many you need for guests and keep that amount. Give away the rest. Also, throw out glass items that are chipped.

- Keep silverware organized within one to two drawers.

- Store cooking and baking utensils in a drawer if you have room for them instead of in a container on the counter. Your counter will look neater with utensils stored away.

- Check the expiration date of all food products and throw out those that are past due.

- Store all spices together. I like using a decorative spice rack organizer and keep this next to my stove on the counter. I keep the extra supply of spices in my freezer to keep them fresh. I have one shelf in there reserved just for spices and I keep them neatly lined up in zip lock bags or in the jars they came in. You may also choose to store spices in a spice organizer that rests in a drawer or keep them altogether in a cupboard in one basket. When you cook all you have to do is take the basket off the shelf and select the ones you need. Remember to put everything back when you are done.

- Keep teas, coffee and hot cocoa mixes in one area. I like to use a decorative tea box for my tea bag packets so I have that on display instead of in a cupboard. Once you fill the tea box, keep the extra teabags that don't fit inside in one large zip lock bag and store that, then refill the box when needed. You can also choose to put the tea bag packets all in a decorate basket. This can easily be taken from its storage area and placed on the table for your guests who come for tea. By using a box or basket, you save yourself time and the hassle of searching through a collection of boxes in your cupboard to find the right one, and trying to catch half of them as they fall out in the process. Loose teas can be kept in their packages and altogether in one basket in the cupboard or use labeled glass jars for each.

- Designate one cupboard for snack items, cereal and crackers.
- Cut down the cereal boxes when the supply goes down so that you can stack them on top of each other to make use of vertical space.
- For all snacks such as chips that come in large bags, cut down the bags once the supply inside starts shrinking and use an elastic or bag clip to secure them closed. Store the bags standing up on their side (like standing tubes) in a plastic storage bin that would fit them all. When you want a snack, you just have to pull out the bin and choose what you want. If there is not enough vertical space in your cupboard to stand up the bags, just lie them down instead.
- Remove individually packaged snack items such as cookies, granola bars and fruit roll ups from their boxes and keep them altogether in a storage basket. Your children can easily select the snacks they want as they look inside instead of having to find the correct box and then having to rely on them to get the box back into the cupboard in the correct spot. When it is time to go shopping, you also do not have to waste time looking inside each box to see how many snacks are

left. It will be much easier to get an idea of what you need to buy as you look at the collection in the basket.

- Keep all canned foods together.
- Keep all dry pastas and rice in one location. Use baskets to separate the packages of pastas from the rice or separate storage containers or canisters for each.
- Keep all food items for baking that are of smaller size together such as sprinkles, chocolate chips, vanilla, baking soda and powder.
- Keep all other items that take up more room such as bags of flour, sugar, salt and all cooking oils in one location. You may choose to keep flours, sugars and other items that come in larger bags in glass storage containers or mason jars instead. If you do not have room in a cupboard for these items, then displaying them in decorative storage containers would add a nice touch on your counter or on an exposed shelf.
- Choose clear glass storage containers for leftovers and for storing other fridge items instead of plastic. Plastic containers can become stained and smelly. Think of how many storage containers you can fit into your fridge and that you realistically would use at one time, and then keep that amount. I recommend using square and rectangular shaped containers instead of round ones so that you use space well in the fridge and in the cupboard. I like to store the containers with the lids on them and then stack one container on top of another. This way I do not have to search for the matching lid. I also choose to hand wash the lids instead of putting them in the dishwasher so that they stay in good shape. Choose a variety of

sizes including very small ones to store small amounts of leftovers which will save space in your fridge.

- Connect with what you want for yourself as far as your health and only choose to keep food items that serve your body well. Get rid of what you feel is unhealthy for you. I believe it is important to have a treat once in a while so make sure you have a few in store; just remember to eat a small amount. A "Queen" practices self-control, so remember this as you take control of the portion you take.

- Always keep your kitchen table clean and clear so that it is ready to welcome its guests for each meal. Display flowers in the centre to make the space feel welcoming and pretty.

- Sweep your floor after the last meal of the day so that it is clean and ready for the next day.

- Allow yourself to have one "junk" drawer to toss small items in that you do not have another place for at the moment. Practice "letting go" and just toss things in. Commit to keeping the "junk" though, to one drawer. Go through the drawer at the start of each new season and clear out what you no longer need. This may be a good place to keep the little toys that come home in loot bags from birthday parties for example. You may want to divide the drawer in half using a divider. Let you kids know that one half is for them and the other for you.

- Keep a neat stack of clean dishcloths in a basket under the sink along with all cleaning products and larger items such as your box of garbage bags.

- Keep all plastic and foil wrap items together.

- Make use of the inside of the cupboard door at your sink by adding hooks to hold dishcloths or screw in a storage shelf for whatever you choose to keep there.
- Store all cookie sheets, pizza trays and other large items used for baking in the drawer below the oven along with your oven mitts. You may also want to store trays upright on the floor between the counter and fridge for example, if you have no other space available.
- Select a storage space in your home to keep your supply of paper towels, napkins and tissue boxes.
- Keep paper plates, cups and plastic cutlery together.
- If you have a formal dining room then collect all items that you enjoy using in that space and store them in the cabinets you have there, such as fine china, wine glasses and wine bottles.

As I wash my dishes, I feel my fears washing away.
As I wash each dish, I make a wish.
When I wash and put away what I see, I am able to stay clutter-free.
I enjoy staying present as I prepare my food.
As I eat from my plate I remember how the Universe serves me with wonderful surprises.
As I hold my cup I remember that mine is overflowing with everything that is good.
As I use a knife I remember to cut out thoughts that bring me down.
As I chop and slice I remember to break up my tasks into manageable chunks.
As I peel the skin off the fruit, I peel off my layers of self-doubt.

As I hold my spoon I remember to scoop out what I don't want in my life, in order to make room for what I do want.

I hold onto my fork after the main course remembering that the best is yet to come.

I choose wisely what I put in my mouth, just as choose wisely what I place in my mind.

I fill my bowls with an abundance of joy.

As I boil water I remember that it all boils down to these choices: To trust or not to trust that I live in a Universe that is fully supportive and loving; and whether to follow my inner "Queen's" guidance or not.

I hold up the frying pan and shout "Yes I can!"

As I use my spices I remember that I love to spice up my life through my feminine.

As I look at and eat apples I remember that I am strong in my core.

When sitting at the table I remember that I am always in go(o)d company.

As I appreciate the flowers on the table I remember my growth.

I am served good thoughts at each meal.

I am living a delicious life.

Your Family Room

The family room is the place for you to relax on your own, and enjoy times together with family, guests and your pet. Make this space most inviting. This is one location where it is nice to display pictures of those you love along with objects that align with who you are, your dreams and with what is important for you and your family. Select one area to begin to declutter and then start! Choose either a cupboard space, all furniture surfaces at once, a set of shelves, the couch or any area that has a pile of things. Remember to remove everything that belongs in another room at the end of your decluttering session. Put those items in their designated spaces and if you do not yet have that area decluttered, then remember that it is ok for now to keep the items in a little pile.

- Use wall space to hang collections of photographs. By doing this you create more space for other items to be placed on furniture surfaces instead of having them covered with many frames.
- Store CDs, DVDs and family/adult board games in a cupboard.
- Keep couches and chairs clean and free from clutter.
- Keep reading material in a magazine rack or in a neat stack on the coffee table.
- Keep children's toys in one area if you do not have another room in the home that you designate as a playroom. Use baskets, a chest or plastic drawer systems to keep toys organized. Store items together by category (e.g. all Barbie dolls together with their clothing, all little pieces of furniture for playhouses together, all racing cars, building blocks, etc.). By doing this your children can grab the basket or drawer they need and take it to their play area. This will keep all other toys clear from their play space. Your children will enjoy what they have much more as they use their toys this way rather than having all the toys they own spread out across the floor. This causes a lot of distraction. You can even rotate the toys they

use by storing some away and then rotating every few weeks. They will be excited about having something different to play with when you rotate; and by keeping the toys in order you teach your children how to categorize and organize.

- Boxes of chocolates and other sweet treats you like to serve to your guests can be stored in a cupboard instead of always on the coffee table so that you are not tempted to eat them at any time. Take the treats out before your guests arrive.

It's a real treat, to sit where it is neat.

I appreciate all who are in my life and create a beautiful space for them to sit in.

My children know that everything they play with has a space to rest when not in use.

To relax here is such a pleasure, a cozy organized space to treasure.

My clean and comfy couch loves to receive me, and feels so good to rest on to just "be."

I love entertaining guests in my space that is organized, pretty and free from clutter.

I feel support from the beautiful objects that are surrounding me here.

My pet loves being in this fresh and clean space.

Your Home Office Space

Whether you designate one room as your office or just use a small area in another room (such as in the kitchen, a closet space or desk in the family room), make this a place you enjoy coming to. Allow it to be your space to receive creative inspirations and new ideas. Keep the area as neat as you can, with lots of open spaces so that you feel relaxed when there. In the previous chapter I gave you suggestions on how to file your papers, creating sacred spaces for them; therefore, paper clutter will not be discussed again here. I just recommend that you create the sacred spaces for your papers first and then declutter the rest of the office space. Choose to clear one area at a time such as the entire desk surface, all shelving in one area, a couple of drawers at a time or a pile of things that are lying on the floor in one area.

- Small office supplies can be organized in baskets in a drawer. Group like items together. Keep as much as you can off the surface of the desk.

- Make sure that you clear your entire desk at the end of each day to let the Universe know that you are ready to receive new opportunities, inspirations and great surprises the next day. Close your daily planner and put any books or papers you are working on in a neat pile to one side.

- If you do not have space for your filing cabinet in your office area, then store it in another location and make sure you can get to it easily so that you can easily file papers at any time.

- Keep all reference books related to your business in one area.

- Store extra office supply items in a location that is not right at your desk. Only keep things around the desk that you use and refer to regularly.

I prefer to have more space open for items that are used regularly in the office area and in my children's bedrooms where they have their desks and so I use my cold cellar to store extra office and school supplies. One part of that room is designated for the office supplies and the other for the baking/entertaining kitchen items I discussed earlier. I keep the extra supplies organized like a store does; paper products are together, binders, etc. Everyone in my home knows where to go when they run out of something at their desk. They do not mind the walk to get what they need.

There is less clutter in my mind when things are easy to find.
Each inspiration is a treasure, and I take inspired action with pleasure.
To invite new opportunities to this place, I make sure that there is space.
When I do one task at a time, I always feel fine.
I do what I love as I sit at my clutter-free desk.
I do know that with clutter removed there is flow.
To avoid another pile, I commit to file.
The Universe does its part, as soon as I start.
At the end of the day, I store all away.

All Remaining Spaces In Your Home

From what you have learned here you can now create so many beautiful sacred and organized spaces in your home. I know that you will be able to continue decluttering the locations that still need attention, and are not mentioned in this book, on your own with ease. I mean areas such as your attic, basement, garage, linen closet and laundry room to name a few. I have purposely not covered how to declutter every possible storage space or room in your home because at this point I want you to take over and practice all you learned and use your own creativity to get organized in the remaining places. I want you to feel empowered from what you learned and see what you can do just by listening in, instead of listening to the words I express here. Trust that you have all answers within, because you do.

You may enjoy reciting what is below as you declutter all remaining rooms and also think of this as you enjoy the beautiful sacred spaces you have already created:

I practice detachment from the objects in my space at the same time as feeling how they support me. I practice attachment to self-love and believe in my dreams. I practice detachment to the outcome of my dreams as I trust and have complete faith that I am receiving what I wish for... or something even better.

My sparkling, magnetic "Queen," you have now read all I have to say about getting the clutter out of your life! Now is the time to take in everything you read and make the decision as to when you want to start to take action! I hope that it is really soon!

I know that I have given you a lot of information to absorb. Trust that you will always be prepared in the best way possible as you move through the clutter in each space. During one decluttering session you may recall what you learned about being in your feminine and you will transmute this energy into decluttering power. Remember that the feminine is the energy of transformation. To stay on task and follow routines, remember too, the importance of getting into your masculine. In another session you may remember some affirmations which will help you stay strong and positive as you let go of items that no longer fit in your life. In the next session you may become inspired to have sexy visualizations about you with the partner of your dreams, and connect to how you feel as your love expresses their desire for you as you sort through your lingerie for example; and this will drive you to do even more. See yourself as a gift... your partner's gift. When you are feeling stuck, just turn to your inner "Queen," this book and the accompanying workbook for inspiration and guidance. Also make sure to reach out to others for support, as this is important to do too.

When you feel that you have done most of the work to get the clutter out of your home and are ready to create the most meaningful living spaces that bring out all of your best parts even more, then you are ready for the final chapter! You should feel so incredibly proud of yourself for taking the bold brave step to clear your clutter and at the same time become the most valuable feminine woman filled with love that you can be! I am so proud of you! Now is the time to celebrate for all that you have done and all of who you are!

To continue the celebration of loving all of who you are and at the same time as decorating your beautiful home now that the clutter is out, I suggest you take your final royal steps I am requesting you to take, into the final chapter. As the "Queen" of your life you deserve to live in a "Queendom." Your home is now going to become this...

CHAPTER 11
You Will Decorate Your "Queendom" To Honor These 12 Things

Given that you have removed all of the clutter from your sacred spaces and have joined them together, I want you to envision them holding hands. By doing this your home is now fully ready to support you in all that you desire in your life! You have now created your inner and outer home to serve you so well. I hope you have enjoyed the process to this point and feel really good with all that you have accomplished! You have done so much and perhaps it is at this time that you have found what you love to do and your purpose that was hiding under all of your stuff!

You are the "Queen" of your home and of your life and I want you to be reminded of this every day, so I am giving you some of my favorite decorating suggestions that you can use in order to remember your best qualities while you are at home. It will be powerful when you give meaning to objects in your space as you set the intention of what each object means to you. My life changed in amazing ways as I did this myself and yours will too! Remember, your thoughts help create your world so if you attach thoughts that make your heart and soul sparkle with joy, to what is around you, your possessions will support you. You will all of a sudden be triggered to think about things that feel wonderful and supportive to you as you look at what is displayed in your home and how objects and furniture are placed. You can give any meaning you want to any object. You can use some of my suggestions and also add your own. Remember too, the importance of clearing out subconscious beliefs that do not align with who you are, and replacing them with new ones that support you.

The ideas presented below come from what I learned living in my parents' home where some Feng Shui principles were practiced, what I learned and tried in my own homes after reading further about Feng Shui design and from my own creativity. I have been following some of these suggestions for years and I know they have been powerful for me. You will also see how others in your home will benefit in a wonderful way as they live in a home that has been decorated by a "Queen."

This is the time for you my "Queen," to shine your ruling powers over your home and divinely decorate through your radiant heart and spirit! Make your "Queendom" shimmer with your magical energy and become the beautiful reflection of who you are, as you honor all the parts of you and what is important to you in your life!

When you are done, you may want to continue decorating with other members of your family (if you have others living with you at home), and have them think of what they would like to do to bring out the best parts of themselves too! For now though, I want the focus to be just on you. You will see below that I included several affirmations with the decorating suggestions. Write down the ones that you like and some of your own in my free workbook that you can download at www.divinedeclutteringbook.com.

This is what you will do to honor...

Your Feminine Beauty And Self-Care

- display books that connect you to your feminine (e.g. books on fashion, decorating, gardening, self care, personal growth)
- display paintings of groups of radiant women
- drape a long lace table runner across your dresser or on your coffee table
- display your nail polish bottles on a silver tray
- display bottles of your favorite essential oils and parfumes in your bedroom
- keep fresh flowers in your private sacred space, on your kitchen table and on your desk
- display a container of pretty pens and notepad with a decorative cover on your desk
- decorate with soft fabrics, pillows and some floral patterns
- use tablecloths with soft feeling and delicate prints
- keep a sexy looking pair of slippers by your bed
- play music that brings out the different energies of your feminine ... music that makes you feel inspired, soft, sexy, sensual, relaxed, romantic, erotic, creative, energized, powerful, free

- create a neat pile of luxurious towels to keep by your tub or shower
- display your favorite massage lotion and moisturizer in decorative containers
- display statues or pictures of naked beautiful women in your bathroom
- hang your favorite robe, piece of lingerie and sexy outfit in your closet in a way so that you see these three items easily
- keep your lipstick and other make-up in a fancy pouch that can easily be taken with you in your purse
- display fashion inspired pictures
- display jewellery on an elegant stand or interesting wall hanging of pretty hooks
- hang an attractive apron somewhere in the kitchen
- display affirmations that express something about and honor your feminine and self-care such as these:

I spend time on self-care every day.
I am radiant from the inside out.
I love to strip myself of my masks and to just be me.
I am beautiful on the inside which is reflected on my outside.
I feel feminine and sensual being present in the moment.
I love and treat my body with respect.
I take care of myself to feel my best every day.
I relax in the beautiful spaces I've created at home.
I am sacred and treat myself and my home this way.
I love feeling feminine in my fabulous home.

Your Unconditional Love

- display photos of family and friends
- display your children's art around your home
- keep special letters and photos from friends in a decorative box next to your land line or cell phone in order to stimulate further friendships to come
- decorate with red and pink
- display objects and images with hearts
- display paintings that bring feelings of love
- display affirmations that express something about your unconditional love such as these:

I am so loved.

I love who I am unconditionally.

I respect what I feel in my heart.

I love what I do for myself each day.

I love and appreciate those in my life.

I honor, embrace and love my feelings, and express them freely.

I am open to seeing all of who I am and loving all of me.

I am responsible for my own happiness, and share this with others.

I am grounded in love, faith, my truth and my purpose.

I do everything out of love.

I take care of myself first before I do for others so that I am always at my best.

I am love.

Love radiates out through my heart to reach others.
I am like a light and shine brightly onto others to help them do the same.

Your Compassion

- display books that are about people that stand for world peace or compassion and remove all gossip magazines (as many articles do not show compassion for the people featured inside)
- display objects, images and paintings that bring thoughts of peace to mind and remove those objects and paintings that relate to war or fighting
- have toys and games that can be played peacefully with others and remove toys and games that relate to war or fighting
- collect coins for a charity in a decorative container and keep loose change in your car in order to be ready to give to someone in need
- always have a bag ready to fill with items to donate
- have signs displaying messages on your children's bedroom doors that feel welcoming (e.g. "Only Smiles Allowed Inside") and remove the judgmental and unfriendly ones (e.g. "Keep Out")
- use soft lighting at night
- use soft bedding that feels wonderful to your skin
- make furniture comfortable to sit on with luxurious pillows
- create a warm atmosphere around you while in the bathtub with soft lighting or candles
- decorate with warm tones of yellow to remember the sun and the loving energy it radiates

- display affirmations to express something about your compassion such as these:

I care for myself and for others.

I give without expectations.

I communicate with others with an open mind and open heart.

I speak using kind words.

I donate to others what I no longer need.

I give my time to others in meaningful ways.

I take care of my body as I rest.

My home is warm and welcoming.

I take care of everything and everyone in my home.

I treat my pet in the best loving way.

Your Power

- have comfortable seating fit for the "Queen" that you are
- have seating arrangements created so that wherever you sit you see the entrance; you can greet others into your space and are always aware of who is entering
- place your bed so that you see the entrance when you are lying down and if this is not possible, hang a small mirror so that you can see the door
- choose chairs with a high back so that you feel you are sitting on your throne and are empowered

- use large decorate pillows behind your head as you sleep or use a headboard to feel that your bed is supporting you in your power
- avoid chairs with slats in the back, or cover them with soft cushions
- raise your mattress off the floor
- display pictures and objects that bring feelings of power to you such as mountain scenes and plants with large beautiful flowers
- hang images of people that represent power to you, or have similar goals as your own
- display statues that represent power
- display your "My Life In Pictures" book and vision board (if you made one)
- place your photo on the front of a magazine cover
- stack large luxurious towels in your bathroom
- display affirmations that express something about your power such as these:

I am empowered.

I am a powerful manifestor.

I choose my thoughts wisely.

My "Queendom" supports me in my power.

I am the powerful "Queen" of my life.

I am responsible for what I bring into my life.

I have an abundance of energy.

I am grounded and feel how to go with the flow.

I use my power wisely and only in respectful and loving ways.

Your Love Relationship

- display items in pairs to send out a message to the Universe that you want to be in a relationship and feel yourself in one
- have photos and pictures in your home displaying romantic couples to stimulate a relationship or to remember and appreciate the relationship you are in
- display photos of your partner's loved ones to show that they are welcome in your home
- only display photos of yourself when with at least one other person to remember that you are loved by others and want a relationship if you are not yet in one
- place things in your space that remind you of love in order to attract a romantic partner such as a pair of candles, special notes or a book, pink or rose flowers, and a painting or statue of a loving couple
- display items in red to remember your passion and fire within
- display affirmations that express something about your love relationship or the one you want such as these:

I prepare for my partner by creating the best love relationship with my own self first.

My heart is wide open to give and receive love.

I am open to receiving the greatest love and know that I am worthy of this.

I am in the best healthy relationship that serves me well.

I love my partner unconditionally, just as I love all of myself this way.

I feel safe to be vulnerable with my partner.

I appreciate and respect my partner.

I am loved for being authentically me.

I love to receive and give affection.

I am open to receiving what my partner wants to do for me and give to me.

I share my life with the person I love.

I feel cherished, treasured and adored.

I am in a fully supportive and loving relationship.

Your Good Feeling Thoughts

- allow the sunlight to enter your home as much as possible by keeping windows clean and window coverings open in the daytime
- open windows at any time for fresh air, before you meditate and when you sleep to imagine your thoughts, wishes and dreams moving out into the Universe
- have everything in working order in your home and remove broken objects as they may bring out feelings of broken relationships and experiences
- repair what needs to be fixed as soon as possible
- remove images that bring sad or dark feelings to you (e.g. dark skies, storm scenes)
- keep house clean of dust and spider webs
- make sure all light bulbs are working to remind yourself that you shine bright throughout each day

- decorate with white to remember your pure and light spirit
- bring light into all dark corners of each room
- place sea salt in the corners of rooms or in spaces that you feel you want to cleanse from old/unwanted energy and keep it there overnight or until you feel that energy has left
- use sage to cleanse the energy of a space at any time
- spray natural lavender in areas that you feel need to be freshened up and cleansed
- continue to declutter and organize your spaces so that they always feel aligned with your best self, what you want and bring good feelings to you
- display flowers in a clear vase to represent clarity and transparency, remembering to see and accept all the parts of you
- display sparkling crystals to remind yourself to continue to remove mind clutter on a regular basis and to remember the clarity of your thoughts
- display affirmations that express something about your good feeling thoughts such as these:

I feel fresh and pure.
I am rejuvenated.
I say "YES" to me and to being the best version of myself.
My light within shines outward.
My home always has a fresh scent.
I live in a bright and happy space.
Everything is working in my home.

I let go of what no longer serves me well.

I take care of my thoughts.

I take steps to feel better and better as I acknowledge what does not feel good.

Your Wisdom

- display books that inspire you at home, work and in your car and perhaps keep a small one in your handbag
- play your favorite music that inspires you
- place images of things or people that have important meaning for you
- place images of someone you admire, learn from and feel supports you
- display and light candles to connect with your inner wisdom
- display your beautiful journal and write in it regularly
- display crystals to represent your clear wisdom and to also remember to ask the Universe for answers when you need help
- display affirmations that express something about your wisdom such as these:

I am intelligent and creative.

I am open to receiving new ideas.

I am always provided with what I need to know.

I practice patience.

Answers come to me easily and effortlessly.

I learn from all experiences in my life.

In my heart lies my truth.

I am open to receiving wisdom from Divine intelligence.

I ask the Universe questions and am open to receiving the answers.

I ask for help when I need help.

I appreciate everyone who teaches me new things.

I get inspired from the beautiful music I play in my home.

I acknowledge and listen to my inner "Queen."

I take inspired action.

Your Confidence

- display images that make you feel empowered in your life (e.g. awards, trophies from your past)
- display complimenting letters and photos where you were given special recognition
- create a magazine or book cover with your photo on the front
- hang beautiful mirrors to be able to look at your reflection and feel your confidence growing
- decorate with objects that are a color connected to royalty such as dark blue to remind you that you are the "Queen of Confidence"
- display dark blue pillows on your bed to remember to fall asleep and wake up with the confidence to continue to follow your inner "Queen's" voice of wisdom and love
- display affirmations that express something about your confidence such as these:

I am completely capable to regularly declutter my home.

I am confident.

I know when it is time to let the useless things and thoughts go.

I love to visit myself in the mirror.

I am always wearing my invisible "Crown of Confidence."

I am in control of my life and create what I want.

I am appreciated by others for who I am.

I am free and confident to be the person I want to be, despite what others may think or say about it.

I have complete faith that I am receiving all I dream of and/or something even better.

I live my life how it feels best to me to live, and unapologetically.

I am enough.

Your Spirit

- display and light candles
- have fountains with some movement such as a spinning ball or wheel to remember the forward flow of your life
- display objects and images that remind you of your spiritual support system such as angels, loved ones that have passed on, teachers
- display objects from nature such as stones, crystals, butterflies, wood carvings to remember life force and energy
- display images of hearts and objects that remind you of self-love such as heart shaped soaps

- display books that inspire you to connect to the truth of who you are
- display affirmations that express something about your spirit such as these:

I am love.

My higher power loves me.

I am true to and respect my soul.

I respect and love nature and its beauty.

My life flows forward in a beautiful way.

I am always supported by those I feel in the non-physical.

I always listen in for answers.

I take care of my spirit by being true to who I am.

My home supports what my spirit needs.

I let go of control and fly like a butterfly to my sacred location to rest, wth complete trust that I am supported in life. I am open to allowing for the perfect things, experiences and people to come to me.

Your Prosperity

- fill an envelope with money and stick it on top of the door or entrance way to one of your rooms so that every time you pass through you remember that you are always prosperous
- display a golden piggy bank at your front entrance and fill it up
- place a piece of paper in each of your empty handbags with an intention around abundance

- create a fake bill of an amount of money you imagine having to spend, and place it inside your wallet
- make a check written out to you from the Universe for an amount of money you always want in your wallet, and keep it in there
- display a decorative container for loose change that you collect for donation
- have a large bag out for items that you will donate, knowing that you have an overabundance of things and are ready to give some items away
- only display and keep things that are in good working order
- display affirmations that express something about your prosperity such as these:

I am overflowing in abundance.

I am worthy of being prosperous.

I am always provided with what I need.

I accept what comes to me gracefully and with appreciation.

I always give generously.

I share my wealth and success.

I spend my money wisely.

I do good for others.

I am thankful for the abundance that comes, as I do what I love.

I am open to receiving and ready to receive a huge money gift today.

Your Gifts And The Present

- display small gift boxes to remember to be thankful for the gifts you receive each day

- display a clock without numbers to remember to stay present and that there is only now
- display a figure in a yoga position to remind you of your breath and where you are at this moment
- display a little notebook where you write down daily synchronicities, all the gifts you have received and what you are thankful for
- display candles and light them to connect you to the present moment
- keep two beautiful large cushions on the floor to remind you to sit there and meditate at times you need to become present as you let go of thoughts from the past and worries about the future
- display affirmations that express something about your gifts and the present such as these:

I live in and appreciate this present moment.

I take time to meditate each day in my sacred space.

I am open to receiving what I've asked for.

I am thankful for everyone and everything in my life.

I am ready to receive a glorious gift today.

I wonder how the Universe will surprise me today?

I am so thankful for this day.

I am thankful for my past because of what I've learned.

I go through my day gracefully and with ease.

I become silent in order to hear the answers to my questions.

Your Creativity

- display books that inspire you to do something creative with your hands
- display creative work of yours and your children
- create a small space to do crafts
- design an interesting mobile that feels magical to you (e.g. something that displays some affirmations, has feathers, sparkling crystals) to hang in your home
- decorate using the color purple
- decorate the front of a notebook and use it to write down your creative inspirations
- display affirmations that express something about your creativity such as these:

I give back to the Universe by using, and expressing my creative power.
I am a creative being.
I love what I create.
I am the "Queen of Creativity."
I take time out for me each day to do something fun.
New ideas come to me with ease.
I love my sacred space to create in.
I wake up inspired to do something different.
My home displays my creative gifts.
I share my creative gifts to inspire and help others.
My purpose will become clear as I do what I love.

I love how my purpose is woven into my life.
Doing what I love and just being me, makes me feel beautiful.
I enjoy being creative in how I decorate my home, and love feeling how
the contents inside support me.

Perhaps you will think of some other parts of yourself or of your dreams that you want to be reminded of each day and continue to decorate further. Ask your "Creative Queen Spirit" for suggestions on what to do and then take action! There are no right or wrong answers...just enjoy your magical creative expression!

Conclusion... Final Wishes For The Queen Goddess

You have reached the end of all I have to share with you for now. I would love to hear from you to know how my book and workbook have helped you! Now that you have confidently completed your elegant and feminine flowing walk through these pages, I expect that you will continue to walk oh so gracefully and with your royal crown upon your head through the rest of the pages of your life!

May you enjoy the delicate dance and expression of both your inner masculine and feminine energies as you live each day, and as you continue to practice the sensual art of decluttering. Always remember that taking the best care of you includes taking care of your inner and outer homes. This is your divine responsibility. My hope is that as you decluttered, that not only did you become more organized and create meaningful sacred spaces, but that you found what you enjoy doing and your life's purpose. Most importantly though, I hope that you discovered the most sacred and priceless treasure in your home ... You.

You are the creator, ruler and "Queen Goddess" of your life and now have become the ruler over your "stuff"! Remind yourself of this each time you look into the mirror. Also remember when looking into the mirror and standing there naked, to let go of all thoughts of who and what you think you should be, and instead just "be," and fully embrace, love and accept the true authentic beautiful you that you see in front of you. I wish for you to live the most love-filled, joyous, healthy, authentic, unapologetic, exciting, sensual, successful, creative, confident, peaceful, spiritually fulfilling, abundant, clutter-less life!

Choose to feel your best each day, appreciative and thankful for where you are and all you have in your life right now. Also believe that your dreams are becoming your reality. Give your dreams a heartbeat and see them moving towards you as you take your brave and divine steps to move towards them. May your "Queendom" and everyone in your home always bring you joy. May you always remember to live in a heart-centred way, surrender to your inner voice, see life through eyes of love instead of fear, shine your magnificence and light on others so that you brighten parts of themselves they may need to see, and leave sparkles of your authentic feminine radiance and unique gifts wherever you may go.

With all my love, Aimee

www.ingramcontent.com/pod-product-compliance
Lightning Source LLC
Chambersburg PA
CBHW060005100426
42740CB00010B/1406